ABBA

THE MUSIC STILL GOES ON

THE COMPLETE STORY
BY PAUL SNAITH

Published by Castle Communications Plc
Book Division, A29 Barwell Business Park
Leatherhead Road, Chessington, Surrey KT9 2NY

Copyright © 1994 Castle Communications Plc

Design: Brian Burrows

Thanks to The Official Abba Fan Club, Pictorial Press Ltd and
London Features International Ltd for their help with this project

ISBN 1-898141-35-5

ABBA 1

ABBA

ABBA

INTRODUCTION

ANNI-FRID LYNGSTAD, BENNY ANDERSSON, BJORN
ULVAEUS and AGNETHA FALTSKOG are quite simply, four of
the world's most successful musicians.

During the Sixties they established themselves individually
as major recording artists in their home country of Sweden.

In 1972 they combined their individual musical talents,
together with their first name initials, and created ABBA.
As ABBA, Anni-Frid, Benny, Bjorn and Agnetha reached the
pinnacle of their profession, and within ten years had
established themselves as 'the most successful pop group in
the history of recorded music'. With world-wide record
sales exceeding three hundred and fifty million, ABBA are
one of the greatest legends of popular music.

In 1982 after ten years of consistent success and acclaim,
ABBA disbanded. Anni-Frid and Agnetha embarked on
successful solo careers and worked with a host of respected
and established producers; Phil Collins, Mike Chapman,
Steve Lillywhite, Eric Stewart and Peter Cetera. Benny and
Bjorn continued their music partnership and, together with
Tim Rice, wrote the internationally successful musical
'CHESS'.

Today, Benny and Bjorn are currently writing their second
musical, to be called 'THE IMMIGRANTS'. This, together
with the prospect of some new ABBA recordings in the
future, indicates that the musical talents of Anni-Frid,
Benny, Bjorn and Agnetha are going to be enjoyed for a
fourth decade.

'The Music Still Goes On' is a chronological account
of the lives, loves and achievements of four of the
world's greatest musicians.

I would like to dedicate this, my first book, to the following very special people.

My Family:

Mam and Dad – for all your love and support.

Nan and Grandad – for your geat love and influence.

Sally – for always being there.

Anthony – go for it!

Mick and Katie – two recent and very welcome members to the family, whom I have yet to convert to the sound of ABBA!

Mark 'Nozza' – for being a really 'sound' person, and for being the best friend I will ever have.

Rebecca – my 'second' sister

Karina, Clare, Ian and Matthew – my 'second' family.

Mark 'Gibbo' and Nicky – two very special and unique friends whom I will always remember.

Agnetha, Benny, Bjorn and Frida – for making my life so much happier with ALL of your music.

Many thanks to the following people:

Barbara Craig, Frank Hudson, Lars Blomqvist, Bo Madsen, Kim and Lotte, Nanna and Orm, Rene Andersen, Gorel Hanser, Tim Rice, Phil Collins, Terry Blamey, Chris Charlesworth, Caroline Muir, Jill Little, Sue Barker, Joan Fisher, Ninette Williams, Sheila Bishop, Tim Cate and Elaine Paige.

CONTENTS

CHAPTER ONE
ANNI-FRID LYNGSTAD

It is said 'war brings people closer together', a statement that proved to be true for two young people – Synni Lyngstad and Alfred Haase. It was early 1945 in Bjorkasen, a suburb of Narvik in Norway, when a rather shy nineteen year old local girl, Synni Lyngstad, fell in Love with a young man, Alfred Haase. However, this love affair was far from welcomed by the local people, for Alfred was a German soldier who had been posted to the town during the war. Although the war was nearing an end, still fresh in the minds of the local people was the brutality, violence and hatred that the majority of the German soldiers had brought with them when they had occupied Norway some years previously. News of Synni's love affair soon spread throughout Bjorkasen and as it did, Synni was immediately treated as an outcast. People she had known all her life would now spit at her, swear at her, or simply ignore her.

Despite the tremendous pressure Synni endured, her love affair with Alfred continued until the inevitable happened, Alfred was ordered to return to Germany. Before leaving, Alfred promised Synni that he would return to Norway as soon as he could and they would marry. After an emotional farewell, Alfred boarded his ship, leaving behind Synni and unknown to him, their unborn child. On Thursday 15th November 1945, Synni gave birth to a healthy baby daughter and named her Anni-Frid after her grandmother. Still awaiting Alfred's return to Norway, Synni yearned for the day he would return so that they could begin a new life together with their baby daughter. However, that day never arrived, and at the age of twenty-one Synni died – alone, unhappy and broken-hearted.

It was now Synni's mother who had to raise and care for baby Anni-Frid. With the label of 'Tyskbarn' ('German child'), hanging around Anni-Frid's neck, Synni's mother, Anni, decided that it would be best to start a new life in Sweden, where nobody would be aware of their past. This is what she did, and their first stop in Sweden was in a town called Harjedlaen.

One year later they moved to Torshalla, a suburb of Eskillstuna, about one hundred miles from Stockholm. This is where Anni-Frid was raised. It was here, in Torshalla, that Anni-Frid's first appreciation of music began. During the long, dark and cold winter evenings Anni-Frid sat with Anni, whom she now called 'Mamma', and beside the fire the two would sing Swedish and Norwegian folk songs.

"It was Mamma who encouraged me to sing, and it was she who helped me to discover that I could sing" recalled Anni-Frid.

At the age of ten Anni-Frid gave her first public performance at the local village hall, where she sang for a group of children and adults. Her first 'official' performance came the following year, when she sang 'Fjorton Ar Tror Jag Visst Att Jag Var' at a party organised by The Red Cross. At the age of thirteen Anni-Frid was singing professionally in a dance band headed by Ewald Ek at a restaurant in Eskillstuna. Officially, Anni-Frid was too young to be singing professionally in such a place, and so she lied about her age. Anni-Frid's mature appearance and singing technique led everyone to believe that she was actually sixteen.

After leaving the Ewald Ek Dance Band, Anni-Frid joined another band, headed by Bengt Sandlund. Their music was very much jazz orientated, at which Anni-Frid had previously excelled. It was not long before Anni-Frid decided to form her own band together with Bengt Sandlund's bass player, Ragnar Fredriksson. When a further two people joined them the band was aptly named the Anni-Frid Four. During the early sixties, The Anni-Frid Four became quite an attraction in and around Eskillstuna, where they used to perform between four and five nights each week.

At this time, Anni-Frid and Ragnar became more than just friends and, after getting engaged, started living together. On 26th January 1963 Anni-Frid gave birth to a baby boy, naming him Hans. The following year Anni-Frid and Ragnar married and spent their honeymoon on the Canary Islands. At this point it seemed that Anni-Frid's life was safely mapped out for her – primarily as a wife and mother, with her singing providing a welcome contrast.

However, later that same year Anni-Frid entered an amateur talent contest which was held in the neighbouring town of Vasteras. To her surprise Anni-Frid came first in the contest, which gave her the confidence to enter similar contests during the following few years.
It was during these years that Anni-Frid began to realise that singing was becoming a more important part of her life, and so leaving Hans in the capable hands of 'Mamma' Anni-Frid and Ragnar spent much time touring and performing. Anni-Frid also found the time to better her singing technique by training with the well-known opera singer Folke Andersson. By the mid-sixties it became clear that Anni-Frid was becoming more and more ambitious as her signing commitments began to snowball, and these formative years in Eskillstuna provided Anni-Frid with a strong framework on which to build.

Unknown to Anni-Frid, 1967 was going to be the year that would change her life forever. The birth of her second child, Lieselotte, on 25th February 1967, did not hinder Anni-Frid's singing career at all. After winning a talent contest in mid-'67 Anni-Frid secured a place in the national final of a 'New Faces' competition, which was to be held in Stockholm on 3rd

"Anni-Frid is one of our best singers vocally, technically and musically."

September. The song that Anni-Frid chose to sing at the contest was a ballad, written by Osten Warnerbrings, titled 'En Ledig Dag' ('A Day Off'). To her amazement, Anni-Frid won first prize in the contest.

As Anni-Frid was on stage collecting her prize the host of the contest, Lasse Holmqvist, asked Anni-Frid "What will you do tonight?", to which she replied "I will go home to Eskillstuna and sleep." However, the events did not turn out as Anni-Frid expected.   The record company EMI had sponsored the 'New Faces' contest, and as a bonus prize for the winner they had arranged for them to be driven to Stockholm's television studios, where they would appear on the 'live' national chat show, Hylands Horna. That same evening Anni-Frid, the singing mother from Eskillstuna', made her television debut before thousands of viewers.

ABBA 11

Hylands Horna immediately gave Anni-Frid widespread exposure which resulted in a string of recording contracts being offered to her. Anni-Frid decided to accept EMI's offer who quickly arranged for her to record her winning song 'En Ledig Dag', together with her first album. Despite being given widespread exposure via Hylands Horna when released as a single, 'En Ledig Dag' failed to make any impression on the Swedish charts. However, with the release of her debut album, simply titled 'Anni-Frid Lyngstad', Anni-Frid received rave reviews from the music critics: "A solid, thoroughly professional debut album. Anni-Frid's singing is unusually intelligent", wrote the national newspaper Dagens Myheter, whilst Expressen delcared "Anni-Frid is one of our best singers vocally, technically, and musically."

It was at this time that Anni-Frid was faced with a major decision, Stockholm was the place to be if she wished to further her music career. However, Stockholm was also one hundred miles from her home town, husband and children. Could she combine the two? The decision was not made any easier by the fact that Anni-Frid and Ragnar were also at this time experiencing marital problems and had decided to seek a divorce.

After much discussion, Anni-Frid decided to move to Stokholm to better her music career, leaving her two children in Eskillstuna with Ragnar. "I am not afraid of playing second fiddle to Anni-Frid's career. If she has a chance to be successful then she must take that chance. I would never stand in her way. Leaving the children behind was an awfully big wrench for her – everyone could see the sadness in her eyes when she spoke about being away from them" said Ragnar.

In Stockholm Anni-Frid began adjusting to her new life and found herself a tiny, one-bedroom flat which was now her new base. First on Anni-Frid's agenda was a lengthy tour of the popular Swedish 'folkparks' together with Lasse Berghagen. After performing to audiences of five hundred to one thousand people at numerous 'folkparks' throughout Sweden, Anni-Frid began a two year tour of Sweden's nightclubs together with Charlie Norman. "Touring With Charlie Norman was really good schooling for me" recalled Anni-Frid. Slowly but surely, Anni-Frid was becoming a major attraction throughout Sweden.

It was during the tour with Charlie Norman that Anni-Frid first met Benny Andersson in Malmo, early 1969. Anni-Frid was appearing at the Kramer nightclub whilst Benny and his group, the Hep Stars, were appearing at the neighbouring Arkaden nightclub. Although their initial meeting was "rather quick", when Anni-Frid and Benny found themselves sitting on the same panel on the Ake Strommer Midnight Hour radio show some weeks later, they were already acquainted. It was after this radio show that Anni-Frid and Benny agreed to see more of each other and a relationship soon developed. On 18th August 1969 Anni-Frid and Benny became engaged.

By this time, Anni-Frid was becoming a regular visitor to the Swedish album and single charts and her numerous appearances on television had made her a national celebrity. International success also beckoned when she took part in three International Music Festivals – two in Japan and one in Venezeula. However, nothing came from Anni-Frid's participation in these festivals. For international success she would just have to wait a few years longer.

CHAPTER TWO
BENNY ANDERSSON

Through their love and appreciation of playing Swedish folk songs on their accordians, Efraim and Costa Andersson had started the ball rolling. Therefore, when Costa's son Benny was born on Monday 16th December 1946, it seemed inevitable that he would inherit his father's and grandfather's love of music.

Benny was born in Vallinby, a suburb of Stockholm Sweden, where he was raised by his mother and father, sister and grandfather. After showing an early interest in music at the age of six, Benny was given his first accordian and by the time he was ten had progressed to the piano. After having one of two 'rather dull' piano lessons, Benny's father and grandfather intervened and taught him themselves by teaching him Swedish folk songs. From that moment, music took over Benny's life.

Not being overwhelmed by the academic side of school life, at the age of fifteen Benny left school without sitting his final exams. He was finally free to concentrate of music full-time. During the early Sixties Benny was already giving amateur performances on his piano at local youth clubs, and would sometimes be accompanied by a young female singer – Christina Gronwall. During 1962 Benny and Christina began dating, became engaged and on 20th August 1963, their son Peter was born.

During the daytime Benny worked as a janitor at his father's firm, Svenska Bostader, and during the evenings Benny was now the keyboard player in a local band called Elverlerts Spelmanslag. With the band Benny was kept busy playing various clubs in and around Vallinby, earning enough money to support his girlfriend and son. For one particular gig Elverlerts Spelmanslag needed transport, and so the band turned to their mutual friend, Svenne Hedlund, the lead singer in an up-and-coming band called The Hep Stars, for assistance. At the gig Svenne was immediately impressed with Benny's wizardry on the keyboards. Therefore, when The Hep Stars found themselves in need of a keyboard player some months later, Svenne immediately offered Benny the job. "Elverlerts Spelmagslag were on a road to nowhere and I had just finished at Svenska Bostader, so this offer came just at the right time" recalled Benny.

Benny offically joined The Hep Starts in October 1964 and his first recording session with them produced three songs in just one day, 'Cadillac', 'Farmer John' and 'A Tribute to Buddy Holly'. The big break for The Hep Stars came in January 1965 when they were invited to perform one song on the television programme 'Drop In'. The song they chose to perform was 'Cadillac' and The Hep Stars were an immediate hit with the audience. From that moment, The Hep Stars could do no wrong and within weeks they were at number one, two and four on the Swedish chart.

By this time Benny had begun writing his own songs, with 'No Response' being the first one recorded by The Hep Stars. On 25th June 1965, Benny's daughter, Helene, was born. However, despite the birth of their second child, Benny and Christina separated soon afterwards.

Benny's first self-written song to make the charts was 'Sunny Girl' which became one of The Hep Stars' biggest hits, remaining at number one in Sweden for several weeks. After that Benny began writing more and more songs for The Hep Stars, with 'Wedding', 'It's Nice To Be Back' and 'Consolation' all becoming chart hits.

The Hep Stars soon established themselves as Sweden's biggest group. their first three albums and first five singles earned them gold discs, as well as a huge fan following. The great speed at which The Hep Stars had become successful left them all with little time to worry about the business dealing surrounding a top group. Doubled with a lack of sound, financial advice, and a string of 'hangers on' who were only interested in making some quick and easy money, The Hep Stars looked set to hit trouble. Hep House was a production company set up by The Hep Stars, for the Hep Stars. However, the only thing Hep House managed to do was to drain all the band's finances after a series of distastrous business ventures. The most costly of these ventures was a feature film that the Hep Stars had been persauded into making. It was to be called 'Habari Safari' and was filmed in Africa. Backed by their record comapny chief, Ake Gerhard, The Hep Stars spent two weeks in Nairobi, Africa, filming, and then a further ten days in Denmark filming extra footage. In total, five thousand metres of film were used.

Back in Sweden after all filming was completed, The Hep Stars realised that their film had not been scripted, so how could they promote a film that did not have a story. The whole film was scrapped, costing The Hep Stars 280,000 Swedish crowns. The Hep Stars also spent money on a trip to America but did not go, and also hired a recording stuio in London, recording a song that they never released. The Hep Stars soon found that their existing finances were rapidly diminishing.

December 1987 saw the Swedish press reporting that for the past two years The Hep Stars had not paid any tax to the Inland Revenue. The enormous amounts of money that The Hep Stars had been earning, and spending, had now left them with a tax bill totalling 900,000 Swedish crowns. In July 1968 The Hep House Production Company went bankrupt.

Benny's tax debt alone totalled 174,000 crowns, which he managed to reduce to 8,000 crowns after making tough instalments to the Inland Revenue over a two-year period. This, however, was only to lead Benny into receiving a further tax bill for the year 1969, which totalled a further 83,000 crowns. Four years later Benny finally managed to clear his tax debt by sending all the royalties from his songs direct to the Inland Revenue. "I have written for every crown that I owe" said Benny.

"I have written for every crown that I owe."

1969 saw The Hep stars make their last 'folkpark' tour, after which all five members of the group split into two sides. Janne Frisk, Lennart Hegland and Christer Petterson all continued as The Hep Stars, whilst Benny and Svenne Hedlund teamed up with Svenne's singer girlfriend, Charlotte 'Lotte' Walker. Charlotte was already famous in her own right as a member of the American group The Sherrys, who had scored an American hit with the song 'Pop Pop Pop Pie'.

During the years touring with The Hep Stars, Benny had met Bjorn Ulvaeus, who was a member of another successful group called the Hootenanny Singers. Both had built up a strong friendship, and in the summer of 1969 Benny and Bjorn wrote their very first song together. Written after an all night session at Bjorn's father's office, the very first Adnersson/ Ulvaeus composition was called 'Isn't It Easy'. Little did each of them know of what the future would hold.

 16

CHAPTER THREE
BJORN ULVAEUS

Born on Wednesday 25th April 1945, Bjorn Kristian Ulvaues spent the first six years of his life in Gothenburg, Sweden. In 1951 he and his family moved to the east coast of Sweden to a town called Vastervik. Bjorn's mother, Aina, had always been a great lover of music, and so for Bjorn's twelfth birthday she bought him a guitar, hoping that he too would begin to appreciate music. Bjorn immediately fell in love with his present and began to teach himself basic skiffle-orientated tunes.

It was at college in Vastervik that the seventeen-year-old Bjorn and his friend, Tony Roth, were invited by two older students to join their folk band. Calling themselves The West Bay Singers, Hansi Schwartz and Johan Karlberg had found themselves two talented and enthusiastic recruits. Heavily influenced by The Kingston Trio and The Brothers Four, The West Bay Singers soon became very popular with the audiences at local clubs. When college had finished for the summer holidays in 1963, The West Bay Singers travelled across Europe in an old Volvo car, eventually ending up in Spain. By entertaining people along the way with their music Bjorn, Tony, Hansi and Johan managed to make enough money to pay for their food, drink and other expenses.

When they returned to Sweden 'the boys' learned that Bjorn's mother had entered them for a national talent contest. Plats Pa Scen, which was to be broadcast by Swedish Radio during the autumn. The West Bay Singers travelled to Norkopping to sing before the radio's panel of judges, but failed to win any prize. Coincidentally, also competing in the same contest was Anni-Frid Lyngstad.

Despite failing to win a prize, The West Bay Singers were mentioned in a newspaper review of the contest which was read by a talent scout named Bengt Bernhag. Bengt had just formed his own record company, Polar Music, together with his good friend Stikkan 'Stig' Andersson, an ex-school teacher. Bengt and Stig were looking for a folk group that sang in Swedish with a view to signing them to their new record company. After reading the review of the talent contest Bengt approached The West Bay Singers and asked them if they would like to record a demo tape so that he and his partner, Stig, could listen to their music. The West Bay Singers readily agreed and, using equipment from their local radio station in Vastervik, they recorded a demo tape which featured a song titled 'Ave Maria No Morro'. On listening to the tape Bengt and Stig were immediately impressed with what they heard and invited 'the boys' to Stockholm for a formal audition. The result of this formal audition was that The West Bay Singers were the first artists to sign with Polar Music.

Many Swedish groups were at this time performing songs in English, as indeed The West Bay Singers had been, However, Stig felt that the time was right for a group to perform and record in Swedish. 'The boys' took notice of Stig's advice and recorded 'Jag Vantar Vid Min Mila' as their first record. 'The boys' also took Stig's advice about the name of their group. Stig felt that The West Bay Singers was not an appropriate name for four young boys. West Bay had come from the English translation of their hometown of Vastervik. Stig was very interested in the American folk scene and had read many articles about it.

During his reading Stig had come across the word 'hootenanny', a term used by the Americans to describe large folk gatherings. When Stig suggested changing the name of the group from The West Bay Singers to The Hootenanny Singers, everyone was in agreement. With their new name and song, The Hootenanny Singers appeared on a televised talent contest that took place at the television studios in Stockholm. To their great surprise The Hootenanny Singers came first in the contest and 'Jag Vantar Vid Min Mila' became their first Swedish chart success. "We were the only group in the Top Twenty that sang in Swedish" recalled Bjorn. Not only had The Hootenanny Singers scored a huge hit with their first-ever recording, but Polar Music scored its first hit from its first release. However, the immediate attention that surrounds a hit record did not deter Bjorn from his college work, and in the spring of 1966 Bjorn sat, and subsequently passed, all his examinations, as did Tony, Hansi and Johan. Now fully graduated, they performed their first concert at the 'folk park' in Timmernabben, a suburb of Oskarshamn.

For the next two years the Hootenanny Singers toured 'folk parks' during the summer months, whilst during the winter months they recorded and promoted their music via radio and televison. The Hootenanny Singers also started to explore other counties, making six television appearances in Germany, and under the name of Northern Lights released and promoted the song 'No Time' in England, America and South Africa. South Africa was the only country where it made any impression on the charts.

The autumn of 1966 saw Bjorn, Tony, Hansi and Johan begin eighteen months' compulsory National Service. All four were ordered to join the Lifeguards in Linkoping and everyone assumed that this would result in the break-up of The Hootenanny Singers. However, thanks to 'extremely understanding' military chiefs, The Hootenanny Singers were allowed regular leave in order to fulfill their commitments. "We have never worked as hard as we did that year, and we had a mass of hits" recalled Bjorn. The National Service did not interfere with The Hootenanny Singers' popularity, and in 1967 they scored their biggest hit to date by selling 55,000 copies of "En Sand En Gand for Langesen' (The Swedish version of the Tom Jones song, 'The Green Green Grass of Home').

During the Summer of 1967, Bjorn, Tony, Hansi and Johan completed thier National Service. However, instead of continuing full time with The Hootenanny Singers, all four decided to further their education. Tony, Hansi and Johan enrolled at Gothenburg University, whilst Bjorn opted for Stockholm University, where he studied business, law and economics. He also began furthering his knowledge of the music business by working for Bengt and Stig at Polar Music.

Although continuing his involvement with The Hootenanny Singers, Bjorn was beginning to write and record his own songs, as a solo artist, many of which appeared as B sides to The Hootenanny Singers' records. However, in 1968 Bjorn acheived his first real solo success with his own composition titled 'Baby Those Are The Rules', and three further solo successes followed – 'Froken Fredriksson' and 'Raring' (a cover version of Bobby Goldsboro's hit 'Honey'). Bjorn was quickly becomming recognised as a solo artist. During the beginning of 1969, Johan decided to leave The Hootenanny Singers in favour of his family business in Vastervik. Bjorn was also becomming more involved with his solo activities. Therefore the original format of The Hootenanny Singers was disbanded. It was during this time that Bjorn renewed his acquaintance with Benny Andersson, and together the two were becoming quite a serious songwriting duo, already producing some hit records for 'Brita Borg and The Hep Stars'.

"We have never worked as hard as we did that year, and we had a mass of hits."

During the Summer of 1969 Bjorn appeared and sang his solo song 'Tangokavaijeren' on a Swedish television programme. It was at the television studios in Stockholm, during the recording of the programme, that Bjorn met a young female singer from Jonkoping. Bjorn was immediately impressed with the young girl's singing, as well as her good looks. When he began talking to her after the programme, it was obvious that they shared a mutual affection for each other. Enter Agnetha Faltskog.

CHAPTER FOUR
AGNETHA FALTSKOG

It was in a lakeside town of Jonkoping, Southern Sweden, that Agnetha Ase Faltskog was born on Wednesday 5th April 1950. Agnetha's father, Ingvar, was an enthusiastic supporter of the local amateur dramtic society. In his spare time Ingvar organised and staged shows for the local community, with many of the shows containing sketches and songs that he had written himself. It was he who introduced Agnetha to the stage, and at the age of six Agnetha made her stage debut. During 1956, Ingvar staged a Christmas show for the senior citizens of the local community. The highlight of the show came when, during a recital of 'Billy Boy', Agnetha's pants fell down, reducing the audience to hysterical laughter.

By now Agnetha had begun taking piano lessons, and every day she would faithfully go to her neighbour's house to practice on their piano. The following year Agnetha received a piano of her own and, even at this early age, had began to compose her own songs. These early compositions were all nursery rhymes based on the famous Scandanavian Trolls. Agnetha's early flair for music was plain to see, and for the following two years she continued with her piano lessons, as well as playing the harpsichord each Sunday at the local church.

At the age of thirteen Agnetha, together with two friends, began singing, performing together at local venues and staging small tours in neighbouring Smaland. At the age of fifteen Agnetha left school and, after deciding not to further her education, began working as a telephonist at a car sales firm in Jonkoping. It was while Agnetha was working here that she found out that a local dance band, headed by Berngt Enghardt, was looking for a female vocalist. Agnetha immediately applied for the job and after impressing Berngt with her singing was offered the post.

By only performing with the band at weekends Agnetha was still able to keep her job at the car sales firm. However, as the band became more popular, their performances increased and also included week-days as well as weekends. Soon the added performances with the band, together with her job at the car sales firm, became too much for Angetha to cope with. Therefore she needed to make a decision to leave one of her jobs. Agnetha's decision to choose singing made her unpopular at home; however, her mind was made up and for the next to years she was kept busy performing with the Berngt Enghardt Band, as well as making 'guest' appearances with other bands.

It was during this time that Agnetha's break-up with her boyfriend Bjorn Lilja inspired her to write a song that would soon change her life forever. Feeling very unhappy on the day that their romance had ended, Agnetha immediately took herself to her piano and played it in an attempt to forget about her unhappiness. Within an hour of playing Agnetha had picked out a melody and then proceeded to write the lyrics to go with it. The result was 'Jag Var Sa Kar' ('I Was So In Love'), a song telling the story of a young girl's feelings after she had just broken up with her boyfriend. The song could not have been more autobiographical. The song soon found its way into Agnetha's reportiore with the Berngt Enghardt Band, and it was not long before 'Jag Var Sa Kar' became a firm favourite with the audience.

ABBA

Berngt Enghardt had just one ambition and that was to make a record. As chance would have it, a fellow member of Bergnt's band was a relative of a certain Little Gerhard. For many yearls Little had been a famous rock 'n' roll singer in Sweden; however, he had now retired gracefully to the role of producer for Cupol Records. When Berngt sent Little a demo tape of one of his band's performances, Little listened to it but was only impressed with two things – the song, 'Jag Var Sa Kar', and the girl who was singing it.

Within a few weeks, Agnetha received a telephone call from Little. However, Agnetha immediately presumed that it was a hoax, and asked the man if he could prove who he said he was. A few days later Agnetha received a letter from Little, together with the demo tape. Also included with the letter was a signed greeting card from Little, together with an invitation from Little himself for Agnetha to go to Stockholm to record her song. An ecstatic Agnetha finally believed that it was true, but how could she tell Berngt and the fellow band members that Little Gerhard was only interested in her and not them? "This was a tough situation for me. It was very hard for me to break the news to the band, that they would not be on the record." recalled Agnetha.

During the Autumn of 1967 Agnetha took the train from Jonkoping to Stockholm together with her father. On entering Phillip Recording Studio, Stockholm, for the very first time, a very shy and nervous Agnetha could not believe what was happening to her. "It was the most exciting moment of my life. My heart was in my mouth and I had consciously to make my feet take the steps down into the recording room. I then heard all the musicians practising my music – the very notes that I had picked out on my piano. Suddenly I was walking on air and I floated into the room as if I were on a cloud." recalled Agnetha.

During her first recording session, Agnetha not only recorded 'Jag Var Sa Kar' but also a further three songs, one of them being 'Utan Dig' ('Without You'), another of Agnetha's own compositions. On Sunday 28th January 1968, a few weeks after its release, 'Jag Var Sa Kar' entered the Swedish charts at number three. The mass media interest surrounding Agnetha's chart debut resulted in Agentha becoming a national celebrity. Many newspapers devoted larger articles to Agnetha, 'the seventeen year old singer/songwriter from Jonkoping', and a few newspapers made Agnetha's success the headline story.

Agnetha had now signed a recording contract with CBS/Cupol Records, and it was after taking their advice that Agnetha found herself in flat in Stockholm. Alone in her flat Agentha continued to write and record her own songs, with 'Allting Hav Forandrat Sis' ('Everthing Has Changed'), 'En Gang Fanns Bara vi Tva' (Once We Were Two) and 'Om Tarar Vore Guld' ('If Tears Were Gold') all becoming big chart hits throughout Sweden. Agnetha's debut album titled 'Agnetha Faltskog' was also an immediate success and spent many weeks on the Swedish album chart.

A contract with Berngt Enghart's Band compelled Agnetha to tour with them during the summer of 1968; however, as soon as the tour ended on 30th September, Agnetha embarked on her first solo tour of the Swedish 'folk parks'. Her tours, combined with her regular visits to the Swedish charts, soon established Angetha as one of Sweden's leading female singers. Besides her recording and touring commitments, Agnetha also found the time to further her knowledge of the stage and enrolled at 'The Calle Flygare's Stage School' in Stockholm. Agnetha also embarked on a tour of schools in and around the area of her hometown of Jonkoping. The idea of the tour was to help teach children how to brush their teeth correctly.

"It was the
most exciting
moment
of my life."

Agnetha had wirtten a song specifically for the tour, titled 'Borsta Tandtrollen Bart', which she sang to her young audiences at each school. The song was never released commercially; however, copies of it were pressed and given to the schoolchildren. During 1968, Agnetha met and later became engaged to a German songwriter/ producer called Dieter Zimmerman. Agnetha's records were already reaching the German charts and Dieter had promised to help Agnetha achieve big success throughout Germany. Agnetha went to Germany to meet some German record producers who had already chosen the songs for Agnetha to record. Describing their choice of material as 'horrible', Agentha refused to meet the producers' demands and consequently her career in Germany was short-lived. This also proved to be true for Agnetha's relationship with Dieter, and shortly afterwards they ended their relationship.

In early 1969 Agnetha released her new single throughout Sweden, titled 'Zigenarvan' ('Gypsy Friend'). The release of the song was surrounded by much controversy and was described as 'tasteless exploitation' by the national newspapers. The song, written by Agnetha and Bengt Haslum, told the story of a young Swedish girl who was found dancing with a Gypsy, at a Gypsy wedding. By total coincidence, the release of the song had clashed with a very nasty and heated national debate about Gypsies. Even though Agnetha and Bengt had written the song before the debate was even organised, the newspapers in Sweden still accused Agnetha of exploitation.

Another of Agnetha's single releases, titled 'Om Tarar Vore Guld' ('If Tears Were Gold') also generated much media interest upon its release. A Danish band leader, Per Hviid, claimed that Agnetha had stolen the song's melody from him. Then Per intended to sue Agnetha for plagairism. In his claim for damages Per said that Agnetha must have heard his song when he had toured Sweden in 1950. When Per was told that Agnetha was not born until 1950, all charges were quickly dropped.

In 1969 Agnetha released her second album titled – 'Agnetha Faltskog Volume 2'. Its immediate huge success confirmed Agnetha as one of Sweden's top vocalists. In the early Summer of 1969 Agnetha met Bjorn Ulvaeus whilst making a television programme in Stockholm.

When Agnetha further acquainted with Bjorn after the programme she realised that Bjorn was undoubtedly the man of her dreams.

CHAPTER FIVE
TWO COUPLES – ONE DREAM

The break-up of both 'The Hep Stars' and 'The Hootenanny Singers' in 1969 had brought Benny and Bjorn closer together. The two were by this time spending more and more time together, socially and professionally, and their shared musical interests and ideas paved the way for their musical collaborations.

On 18th August 1969, Benny and Anni-Frid became engaged and started living together in a flat in Stockholm. Bjorn and Agnetha had just recently started dating but it soon became obvious that their feelings for each other were becoming stronger each day. The beginning of 1970 saw Anni-Frid and Agnetha continue to pursue their own solo careers and Agnetha released her third album, titled 'Sam Jag Ar' ('On My Own'), which provided her with more success throughout Sweden. Benny and Bjorn were also beginning to establish themselves as a serious songwriting duo. Already their early compositions were making an impact on the Swedish charts, and demand for their songs from other artists was keeping them very busy. The wrote 'Ljuva-60-tal' ('Blissful Sixties') for Brita Borg, 'Spellman' for the three remaining Hep Stars, 'Peter Pan' for Svenne and Lotta, and 'Hej Gamle Man' ('Hey Old Man') for themselves. Benny and Bjorn were also asked to compose the theme music for two Swedish movies, 'The Language of Love' and 'Inga' the latter being the kind of 'adult' movie for which Sweden has became rather notorious.

During April, Anni-Frid, Benny, Bjorn and Agnetha all went on holiday together to Cyprus, and it was here that Bjorn and Agnetha became engaged. Upon their return to Sweden Benny and Bjorn, having now written many new songs together, decided to record a full album by themselves. Using their own names, Bjorn Ulvaeus and Benny Andersson, Benny and Bjorn recorded their first ablum titled 'Lycka' ('Happiness'), at Metronome Studios, Stockholm. The album, also produced by Benny and Bjorn, featured eleven Andersson/Ulvaeus compositions: 'Hej Gamle Man', 'Nanting Ar Pa Vag', Ge Oss En Chans', 'Lieselotte', 'Lycka', 'Kara Gamla Sol', 'Det Dar Med Karlek', 'Volkommen In I ganget', 'Lilla du Lilla Van', Kalles Visa' and 'Livet Gar Sin Gang'. Although uncredited, Anni-Frid and Agnetha appeared on one song, 'Hej Gamle Man', when Benny and Bjorn had invited them to sing backing vocals. Anni-Frid and Agnetha were only too happy to help their fiancés, and therefore 'Hej Gamle Man' is the very first recording featuring Anni-Frid, Benny, Bjorn and Agnetha together. When released in late 1970, Benny and Bjorn's debut album was an immediate success throughout Sweden, which led to Benny and Bjorn performing together at various clubs and nightspots throughout Sweden. 1st November, 1970 saw the debut public performance of Anni-Frid, Benny, Bjorn and Agnetha as a group. Benny and Bjorn had a booking to appear at the Valand Cabaret Restaurant in Tragarn – a suburb of Gothenburg. That particular night Anni-Frid and Agnetha did not have any plans, so they decided to help their fiancés again by performing with them. However, this time Anni-Frid and Agnetha were credited and all four were billed as 'The Festfolk Quartet' (the word 'festfolk' meaning engaged couples). The following day a review of The Festfolk Quartet's performance appeared in the national newspaper 'Expressen', written by Sonya Hedenbratt. It read: "A fast moving and variated entertainment, with some very neat libretto here and there. The Festfolk Quartet are as well-matched on stage as they are off it".

In February 1971, Benny and Bjorn had their first glimpse of international success when they entered one of their songs, 'Livet Gar Sin Gang' ('The Language of Love') in the Malaga Melody Festival. Their song came sixth but, despite not being an overwhelming success, their song was sold to various countries and the famous French singer/actress Francoise Hardy recorded it. Anni-Frid was also hoping for international success when she entered a song for the Swedish heats of the 1971 Eurovision Song Contest. However, she failed to make any impression with the panel of judges and so she began recording her second solo album, titled – 'Frida', which was produced by Benny.

Meanwhile, Agnetha had won a starring role in the Swedish production of the Andrew Lloyd Webber/Tim Rice musical 'Jesus Christ Superstar'. It opened at the Scandavavium in Gothenburg on 18th February, and Agnetha received rave reviews for her portrayal of Mary Magdelene. Agnetha also scored another huge chart hit throughout Sweden when she released the song 'I Don't Know How To Love Him' from Jesus Christ Superstar as a single. After finishing her run as Mary Magdelene in Jesus Christ Superstar, Agnetha teamed up with Benny and Bjorn and the three of them began a tour of the Swedish 'folk parks'. Bjorn and Agnetha had now decided to marry and so the 'folk park' tour provided them with an ideal opportunity to search for a 'right' church for their wedding. "We wanted a fine, old Gothic church, set in lovely countryside", recalled Agnetha.

Bjorn and Agnetha found their church in the village of Verum, a province of Skane in Southern Sweden and, on 7th July 1971, they were married. The wedding brought the village of Verum to a standstill as nearly three thousand people came to seen 'the showbusiness wedding of the year'. Inside the church, the Rev. Uno Wardner conducted the service, whilst Benny finally managed to fulfil one of his ambitions by playing Mendelsohn's 'Wedding March' on the church organ. He also added his own personal touch to the proceedings by playing 'Wedding', a song that he had written and recorded with The Hep Stars.

As Bjorn and Agnetha left the church in an open horse-drawn carriage the awaiting press photographers and well-wishers seized the opportunity to photograph the happy couple, before Bjorn and Agnetha headed to nearby Whittsjohus, where their reception lasted well into the night. The following morning a veil of sadness was cast over the wedding celebrations when Stig Andersson received a telephone call from Stockholm, telling him that his close friend and business partner, Bengt Bernhag, had died. Over the years Bengt had been a 'second father' to Bjorn, and it was Bengt who had taught Bjorn everything that he knew about the music business. After suffering from colitis and long fits of depression, Bengt had commited suicide.

> *"We wanted a fine, old Gothic church, set in lovely countryside."*

This tragedy not only left Stig without a close friend, but had also left him without a business partner. therefore, looking at the situation realistically, Stig immediately asked Bjorn if he would like to take over Bengt's job at Polar Music. Bjorn readily agreed, on the condition that he and Benny could 'job share' the post. Stig agreed and in the Autumn of 1971 Benny and Bjorn became producers for Polar Music. Benny and Bjorn's first assignment at Polar Music was to produce an album for The Hootenanny Singers, titled 'Our Lovliest Tunes – Part Two'. They next produced the debut album for Ted Gardestad, a young up-and-coming Swedish artist.

The end of 1971 saw Anni-Frid, Benny, Bjorn and Agnetha once again combining their invidual musical talents into a single act at a restaurant in Gothenburg. It had been twleve months since they had all performed together as one, and again they received optimistic reviews in the newspapers the following day. However, the time was still not right to make a full time career out of their four individual musical talents. 1972 began with Benny and Bjorn scoring another hit record with 'Better To Have Loved', which was recorded by Lena Andersson. The song was entered for the Swedish heats of the 1972 Eurovision Song Contest. Despite achieving a third position in the contest, 'Better To Have Loved' reached the number one position on the Swedish charts. Lena Andersson was also invited to perform the song at the Japanes Song Festival, which was held in Tokyo. At the festival 'Better To Have Loved' won the first prize for 'best tune', much to the delight of Benny and Bjorn. However, within minutes of the award being presented, the American magazine 'Billboard' threw confusion into the celebrations when they claimed that it was the lyrics to 'Better To Have Loved' that had won first prize. Whether it was Benny and Bjorn's lyrics or tune that had won first prize nobody was quite sure, but what was sure was that Benny and Bjorn had won their first international award as songwriters.

It was at this time that Benny and Bjorn had written enought songs to justify going into the studio to record them. However, this recording session at Metronome Studios was going to be quite different for two reasons. Firstly all the songs had English lyrics, and secondly Benny and Bjorn had invited Anni-Frid and Agnetha to accompany them vocally on all the songs. The recording session produced five new songs – 'People Need Love', 'He Is Your Brother', 'She's My Kinda Girl', 'Santa Rosa' and 'Merry Go Round'. It was after the recording session that things began to snowball for Anni-Frid, Benny, Bjorn and Agnetha after many people who had heard the songs commented on how good Anni-Frid and Agnetha sounded together. First came an offer from a Japanese music publisher who had heard 'She's My Kinda Girl' and wanted the publishing rights to it so that it could be released as a single in Japan, After negotiations with Stig, 'She's My Kinda Girl' was released in Japan under Benny and Bjorn's names. 'She My Kinda Girl' was a huge success in Japan, with sales exceeding 500,000 copies. The attention that this success brought Benny and Bjorn in Japan led them to be asked to submit a song for the 1972 Japanese Song Festival. Benny and Bjorn agreed and decided to submit 'Santa Rosa' as their song. As with the recording of 'Santa Rosa', Anni-Frid and Agnetha also accompanied Benny and Bjorn when they performed the song at the festival in Tokyo. Despite failing to win a prize at the festival, 'Santa Rosa' and Benny, Bjorn, Anni-Frid and Agnetha were given a warm reception by the Japanese audience.

Up until now, Anni-Frid and Agnetha had never been credited for their contribuiton to Benny and Bjorn's records. However, when it was decided to release 'People Need Love' as a single, Anni-Frid and Agnetha's vocals were so prominent that they would have to be given credit. At first Stig disagreed; however, after gentle persausion he agreed to give Anni-Frid and Agnetha credit. Therefore in June 1972, 'People Need Love' was released in Sweden under the title of Bjorn and Benny, Agnetha and Anni-Frid. Within a few weeks of its release "People Need Love' was at number two on the Swedish chart. Under the names of Bjorn and Benny, with Svenksa Flicka (Swedish girls), 'People Need Love' was also released in America by Playboy Records. However, with Playboy Records being a relatively small company, they were unable to press enough copies of the single to satisfy demand. Therefore 'People Need Love' peaked at number 115 on the American charts.

On a personal level, it was during June that Agnetha and Bjorn decided to start a family, and Agnetha fell pregnant.

Following the success of 'People Need Love', Bjorn and Benny and Agnetha and Anni-Frid released a second single in Sweden, titled 'He Is Your Brother', together with 'Santa Rosa' as the B-side. The single soon made an immediate impact on the Swedish charts and was a big success. 'He Is Your Brother' was also released in France and Germany, where it made the charts in both countries. With two single successes to their credit, it was at this time that Bjorn, Benny, Agnetha and Anni-Frid decided to work together regularly, and would write and record songs soley for themselves.

During the winter of 1972 Benny and Bjorn received an invitation from the Swedish Broadcasting Corporation to submit a song for the 1973 Swedish heats of the Eurovision Song Contest. Benny and Bjorn readily agreed, seeing the contest as an ideal opportunity to present their 'new' group to an international audience. In order to do this Benny and Bjorn, together with Stig, needed to compose a song that would have immediate international appeal.

During the Christmas and New Year holidays, Benny, Bjorn, Agnetha, Anni-Frid and Stig spent their time at their holiday homes on an island in Stockholm's Archipelago. It was here that Benny, Bjorn, and Stig began working to compose that all-important song. In January 1973, Benny, Bjorn, Agnetha, Anni-Frid and Stig emerged from their holiday, feeling confident that they had found the song to launch them as international artists. Benny and Bjorn had come up with what they thought was their 'strongest' melody to date, whilst Stig had written a lyric that was 'catchy' and internationally appealing. The result was 'Ring Ring'.

The date of the 'Eurovision heats', 10th February, was fast approaching, so Bjorn, Benny, Agnetha and Anni-Frid did not waste any time in recording their new song. In total they recorded 'Ring Ring' in four different languages, Swedish, German, French and English, the latter version having lyrical input from Neil Sedaka and his partner, Phil Cody. February 10th arrived and Bjorn, Benny, Agnetha, Anni-Frid and Stig all felt confident that 'Ring Ring' would do them all proud. Already, 'Ring Ring' was a firm favourite with the Swedish people; however, their views did not matter, the decision to choose the song to represent Sweden in the 1973 Eurovision Song Contest was entirely up to a 'panel of experts'. Also, the fact that Agnetha was now heavily pregnant presented the press covering the contest with a sideline story. Many people speculated whether it would be the contest for Agnetha or the maternity ward.

Despite the tremendous faith everyone had in 'Ring Ring', together with the great public support for Bjorn, Benny, Agnetha and Anni-Frid, it was not meant to be. The 'panel of experts' had awarded 'Ring Ring' third position. First position went to 'Malta Duo', consisting of Goran Fristorp and Clabbe af Geijerstam.

Although the 'panel of experts' decison had left everyone feeling 'bitterly upset', 'Ring Ring' became an enormous hit, in Switzerland, West Germany, Holland, Australia and New Zealand. On 23rd February 1973 Agnetha gave birth to a baby girl, Linda, at hospital in Stockholm. On 27th February, Bjorn and Agnetha presented their baby daughter to the Swedish press at a press conference held at the hospital.

To coincide with the enormous success of 'Ring Ring', Bjorn, Benny, Agnetha and Anni-Frid recorded their first album together at Metronome Studios, Stockholm. The album, titled 'Ring Ring', featured twelve songs : 'Ring Ring' (Swedish version), 'Another Town Another Train', 'Disillusion', 'People Need Love', 'I Saw It In The Mirror', 'Nina, Pretty Ballerina', 'Love Isn't Easy (But It Sure Is Hard Enough)', 'Me And Bobby And Bobby's Brother', 'He Is Your Brother', 'Ring Ring' (English version), 'I Am Just A Girl', and 'Rock 'n' Roll Band'. When the album was released in Sweden, Bjorn, Benny, Agnetha and Anni-Frid made chart history – the Swedish version of 'Ring Ring' was number one, the English version of 'Ring Ring' was number two, and the album 'Ring Ring' was at number three on the Swedish charts. The album 'Ring Ring' was also released and became a sizeable hit in Australia and some European countries.

The huge success of 'Ring Ring' the single presented Bjorn, Benny, Agnetha and Anni-Frid with the opportunity to visit many European countries including Holland, West Germany, Belgium and Austria. These visits allowed them to promote themselves as a full-time group and also gave them all an insight into how the music business works in other countires. During their visits, Bjorn, Benny, Agnetha and Anni-Frid received a warm welcome in each country, aand they made many friends with music business people who were responsible for promoting their records.

Back home in Sweden the increasing public interest in the group led Bjorn, Benny, Agnetha and Anni-Frid to embark on their first tour of the Swedish 'folk parks'. Dressed in outrageous, glittery costumes, on 15th June 1973, Bjorn, Benny, Agnetha and Anni-Frid gave their first concert at the Liseberg Amusement Park, Gothenburg. The audience and critics loved the show. "The entire show displayed the joyful aim of giving the audience, good, honest entertainment, with a fast tempo and with the kind of music this particular group stands for", wrote Leif Anderson for Goteborgs Posten, whilst Gunner Rehlin, for Goteborg's Tidningen, wrote "Three stars for a good show – a show which, I grant you, is entertaining".

With the release of their new single titled "Love Isn't Easy' in October, Stig began negotiations to launch Bjorn, Benny, Agnetha and Anni-Frid into the two most important and influential music territories – England and America. The American's were not at all interested, whilst in England, EMI, Decca and PYE all refused to contract Bjorn, Benny, Agnetha and Anni-Frid. Eventually a subsidiary of CBS – Epic Records – half-heartedly agreed to contract them. On 12th October 1973 'Ring Ring' was released in England. However, the very little faith that Epic Records had in 'Ring Ring', and Bjorn, Benny, Agnetha and Anni-Frid, resulted in the song's failing to make any impression on England's charts.

It was during this time that Agnetha began to find it increasingly difficult to combine her musical commitments with those of a mother. Therefore it was decided that Bjorn, Benny, Agnetha and Anni-Frid would only perform at weekends. Despite having to turn down over eighty bookings, Agnetha was now free to spend Monday to Friday with her baby daughter whilst Bjorn and Benny were free to concentrate on writing new material for the group. This reduction in performances was also welcomed by Anni-Frid, who had recently lost more than seven kilos in weight due to all the performing and travelling. With Bjorn, Benny, Agnetha and Anni-Frid becoming increasingly more popular, Stig, acting as their manager, found himself talking to the press more frequently. It was during one particular press interview that Stig was to become tired of saying the names of Bjorn, Benny, Agnetha and Anni-Frid in virtually every sentence.

Therefore, Stig decided to take their first name initials, put them together, and refer to them as ABBA. Suddenly the name ABBA seemed to be the ideal name for the group – it was commercially viable and it was a name that could be pronounced easily in any country around the world. From that moment, Bjorn, Benny, Agnetha and Anni-Frid were called ABBA by their audience, introduced as ABBA by disc jockeys, and written about as ABBA by the press. However, before ABBA could be officially launched, Stig needed to seek the approval of one person, Anders Ekstrom. Anders was the director of a long-established Swedish fishing company that traded under the name of Abba. When approached by Stig, Anders did not object to his company and Bjorn, Benny, Agnetha and Anni-Frid trading under the same name. Therefore, ABBA, the pop-group, was born.

By now, Benny, Bjorn and Stig had written enough new material to justify going into the studio to record the very first ABBA album. During October 1973, ABBA began recording their album at Metronome Studios, Stockholm. During November, ABBA, turned their attention to the forthcoming Swedish heats, for the 1974 Eurovision Song Contest, ABBA knew that if their dream of achieving international recognition was to be realsied, then they would have to represent Sweden at the contest. Already at this stage it was widely felt, within the music business circles, that the winning song of the contest would be an up-beat number, as previous winnetrs had recently been ballards. With this knowledge, during the Christmas holidays Benny, Bjorn and Stig worked hard to compose this all-important song. they knew that the song needed to have international appeal. They also knew that the song needed to feature Agnetha and Anni-Frid-s vocals equally. Most importantly, the song would have to make Europe stand up and take notice of ABBA.

1974 began and Benny and Bjorn had composed two equally strong melodies, each of which contained the requirements they needed. It was now up to Stig to find appropriate titles and lyrics to go with the melodies. Searching for inspiration, Stig spent a full Saturday afternoon looking through various books, when suddenly he read a quotation from The Battle of Waterloo. Stig immediately thought that Waterloo would make a great song title and proceeded to write lyrics about it to Benny and Bjorn's melody. Within a few hours the song was complete – lyrics and melody fitted together perfectly.

Leaving ABBA to record 'Waterloo' at Metronome Studios, Stig went to The Canary Islands for a week's holdiay – taking with him Benny and Bjorn's second melody on tape. It was whilst Stig was in Las Palmas that he noticed that the phrase 'hasta manana' was used frequently by the local people, meaning 'see you tomorrow'. Stig immediately thought that 'hasta manana' would make a great song title. As he did with 'Waterloo', Stig proceeded to write the lyrics to 'Hasta Manana' around Benny and Bjorn's second melody. Within hours, Stig had completed a second ABBA song.

Back in Sweden, there were only a few days left before all entries to the 'Eurovision heats' had to be submitted to Swedish Radio. Therefore, ABBA needed to make a decision – would they sing 'Waterloo' or 'Hasta Manana' for Eurovision? Although both songs were equally strong, 'Waterloo' combined the vocals of Agnetha and Anni-Frid, whilst "Hasta Manana' was primarily a solo vocal for Agnetha. With this in mind, Stig decided that 'Waterloo' would be the best song to submit, after telling ABBA that if he was proved to be wrong they could "cut his throat" later.

On Saturday 9th February ABBA performed 'Waterloo' in the Swedish heats of the Eurovision Song Contest. Being judged not by a 'panel of experts' but by 165 ordinary members of the public, ABBA, dressed once again in outrageous costumes, were given a thunderous reception from the audience. The judges were also impressed with ABBA's performance and showed their approval by awarding ABBA 320 points out of the 495 points available. As ABBA celebrated their victory and looked forward to representing Sweden in the 1974 Eurovision Song Contest, to be held in Brighton, England in April, the Swedish press reported ABBA's victory with much publicity. The following morning the Swedish newspapers all made ABBA their leading story and the following headlines could be seen 'The Voice of the People', 'At Last – The Best Song Won', 'This Time The Right Song Won'. Knowing that confidence alone, together with the support of the Swedish people, would not guarantee ABBA the same victory at the Eurovision Song Contest finals in Brighton, Stig immediately began organising a huge promotional campaign for ABBA. Rules stated that no song entered in the Eurovision Song Contest could be released on vinyl until 4th March. This therefore gave Stig just three weeks to deliver a thorough and successful promotional campaign for ABBA.

After making numerous telephone calls to record companies throughout Europe, Stig put together an ABBA promotional package, which included biographies of each ABBA member in different languages, photographs and tape recordings of 'Waterloo'. Then, on Tuesday 12th February, armed with his promotional packages, Stig embarked on a three-day tour of Europe's leading record companies. In just three days Stig met record company chiefs and music publishers in Copenhagen, Amsterdam, Hamburg, Brussells, Paris, Vienna and London. As well as this, two full-page advertisements were printed in America's leading music journals, 'Billboard' and 'Cashbox'.

"The Voice of the People', 'At Last - The Best Song Won', 'This Time The Right Song Won."

This 'all systems go' approach meant that when ABBA arrived in England, during the last week of March, 'Waterloo' was already released as a single and promoted throughout Europe. ABBA's first few days in England were spent in London, where business was mixed with pleasure. Stig's promotional campaign had 'broken the ice' but now ABBA needed to seize every possible opportunity to talk with the international press in person.

CHAPTER SIX
THE BATTLE BEGINS

ABBA's first meeting with the English press came when their music publisher, United Artists, organised a party in London. However, despite ABBA being 6-1 favourites to win the 1974 Eurovision Song Contest, the press were very pessimistic and patronising towards ABBA. When ABBA's odds dropped from 6-1 favourites to 20-1 the following week, the English press wrote about ABBA's "nice song", with one particular newspaper printing a photograph of ABBA with an accompanying caption reading: "No hopers with something to sing about". However, ABBA, remained unperturbed by the press comments, whilst Stig and Benny took advatage of their favourablre odds and placed +10 and +20 on themselves to win the contest.

The setting for the 1974 Eurovision Song Contest was the newly re-furbished Dome Theatre in the popular seaside resort of Brighton, Southern England. On Monday 1st April, ABBA made the hour-long journey from London to Brighton, where ahead of them lay a week of crucial preparation and rehearsal. Together with their 'good luck' mascots (Agnetha's toy donkey and Anni-Frid's black hat) ABBA relaxed and took in the sights of Brighton before rehearsals began the following day. After being issued with security passes the following morning, ABBA entered the Dome Theatre together with the artists and musicians from the seventeen other participating countries. 'Eurovision' rules stated that all vocals must be sung live into the microphone but pre-recorded music backing tapes could be used.

During the first rehearsal ABBA found that their backing track did not sound as it should – it was far too quiet. They immediately asked the English technicians if they would increase the sound of their backing track, but to no avail. As each rehearsal continued each day, ABBA's backing track still remained too quiet. It was only after Stig showed his extreme anger to the technicians on the final day of rehearsals that they responded and increased the volume of ABBA's backing track.

As Friday 5th April came to a close, the tension at the Dome Theatre was high as the all-important day for all the artists loomed. Back at their hotel ABBA cracked open a bottle of champange to celebrate Agnetha's 24th birthday. Relaxing, ABBA reflected upon the past seven days' events, a week filled with rehearsals, photo sessions and press interviews.
As dawn broke on Saturday 6th April, ABBA woke to face the most important day of their lives. There was just one final dress rehearsal at two o'clock before an estimated five hundred million viewers, in thirty-two different countries, would see the finished result. ABBA performed a near-perfect dress rehearsal, and then allowed themselves a few hours of relaxation before having to return to the Dome Theatre in time for the nine o'clock live television braodcast around the world. Benny and Anni-Frid decided to go for a meal at a local restaurant, whilst Bjorn and Agnetha went for a walk around Brighton. Stig, always wanting to be prepared, was in his hotel room practising his 'Thank-You' speech in several languages – just in case of victory.

ABBA

ABBA

Huddled together in a large room backstage at the Dome Theatre, ABBA and their fellow contestants waited nervously whilst Katie Boyle introduced the 1974 Eurovision Song Contest to the world's viewers. Finland were the first country to perform, followed by England, Spain, Norway, Greece, Israel and Yugoslavia – then it was Sweden. As ABBA stepped on stage dressed in outrageous costumes and platform-heeled, silver boots, the audience gave them an encouraging welcome. "All I could think about was the five hundred million people watching us" recalled Benny. As the first few bars of 'Waterloo' played, all nerves disappeared and for the remaining three minutes ABBA gave the most important performance of their career. Three minutes later it was all over. ABA made their way backstage to wait until al the remaining artists had perfomed. Once all performances were given, the judges began awarding their points – five pounds being the maximum award, and zero points being the minimum.

As the judging began ABBA were given a great start when Finland awarded them the maximum five points. After a great start uncertainty crept in, as England awarded ABBA zero points, Spain – one point, Norway – two points, Greece – zero points, Israel – two points, Yugoslavia – one point, Luxemburg – one point, Monaco – zero points, and Belgium – zero points. It was not until The Netherlands awarded ABBA three points, followed by one point from Ireland and two points from Germany, that ABBA could begin to feel optimistic.

With just three countries left to vote, Switzerland awarded ABBA the maximum five points, and it was then that ABBA kenw that they had won the 1974 Eurovision Song Contest. The final one point and zero points, from Portugal and Italy, could not alter the outcome. Swden and ABBA were the clear winners, with twenty-four points – beating second place, Italy, by six points and third place, The Netherlands, by nine points.

Backstage all chaos broke out as the final results were announced. As Agnetha, Benny, Bjorn and Anni-Frid jumped with joy, hugged and kissed each other, their scene of celebration was transmitted live throughout Europe. The 1974 Eurovision Song Contest was now reaching a climax, but not before ABBA performed 'Waterloo' once again. Firstly, however, the song's composers were summoned to the stage to collect their award. As an ecstatic Stig stepped on stage from his seat in the audience, backstage Benny and Bjorn were stopped from reaching the stage by an over-zealous security guard. He told Benny and Bjorn that only the composers were allowed on stage, and not the artists. After much debate, Benny and Bjorn were finally allowed on stage to collect their songwriting award, after they had convinced the security guard that they were the composers and the artists. By this time Stig was already half-way through saying his pre-rehearsed, 'thank-you' speeches in several languages. With all formalities over, it was now time for Agnetha and Anni-Frid to step on stage so that Europe could hear 'Waterloo' one more time. This time, with the pressure off them, ABBA performed a rousing recital of 'Waterloo', unable to hide their obvious delight and excitement.

Now the celebrations could really begin. As champagne corks popped, ABBA were besieged by armies of journalists and press photographers from all over Europe. Questions were asked from every direction – "How do you feel?", "What will you do now?", "Why did you sing in English", "Why do you call yourselves ABBA". In particular, one surprising question came from a Swedish journalist – "Do you realise that 40,000 men died in the Battle of Waterloo?" to which Stig replied, "Why do they have to policitise everything in the news? Wouldn't it be better to congratulate us?" With all questions asked and all photographs taken, ABBA returned to their hotel to change out of their costumes before returning to the Dome Theatre, where they were guests of honour at a party organised by the BBC.

As more champagne was consumed, at 6 o'clock in the morning ABBA finally retired to their hotel. After just three hours sleep, on Sunday morning, ABBA woke and were faced with hundreds of telegrams and letters of congratulations from family, friends and acquaintances. These, together with a string of recording contracts and offers to appear on television throughout Europe, proved without any doubt that ABBA's dream of international recognition had finally come true.

Sunday's activities began with ABBA being guests of honour at The Bedford Hotel where CBS Records had organised a celebratory champagne breakfast. Mixing with friends and media alike, ABBA drank more champagne and answered more questions. Sunday afternoon was spent on Brighton beach, where ABBA held a photo session for Europe's press photographers. However, after a few hours of smiles and poses, ABBA called a halt to the proceedings and retired to the aptly named 'Napoleon Suite' at their hotel. Here, both mentally and physically exhausted, ABBA relaxed, read their telegrams and discussed their immediate plans with Stig.

ABBA's overnight success had resulted in them being offered lots of television work throughout Europe, and each offer needed wise but immediate consideration. Prior to the contest ABBA ha already committed themselves to a television appearance on Dutch TV on Thursday, and also an appearance on German TV on Friday. This therefore left ABBA with three days to concentrate on the English market. The fact that the contest had been held in England proved to be a great advantage to ABBA, for they already had the full attention of the English music press. Had the contest been held elsehwere, it would have proved to be far more difficult for ABBA to attract the attention of the world's most influential music press.

As Monday's newspapers hit the streets, yet more coverage of ABBA's victory could be seen. "The Andersson formula proved a winner, which was certainly helped by the highly professional performance of the ABBA group", wrote The Daily Telegraph, whilst The Daily Express wrote, "ABBA have made a tremendous impression on the English music industry. This is an attractive group. This is a fantastically strong group."
ABBA now turned their attention to the world's leading and most influential music capital, London.

"This is my proudest day in England. You are all fine ambassadors yourself."

As ABBA were driven from Brighton to London on Monday morning, further evidence of their impact was plain to see. 'Waterloo' played frequently on the car radio, and whilst stopping at a garage en route ABBA were besieged by a group of people wanting autographs and photographs.

From their hotel in London ABBA prepared themselves for two days of solid promotion, which would include interviews, televsion appearances, photo sessions and radio interviews. Firstly, ABBA visited the BBC TV Studios, where they performed 'Waterloo' for Top of the Pops. This was then followed by a string of radio interviews for the BBC and numerous independent stations.

ABBA

Tuesday was spent with press photographers. Firstly, ABBA went to Waterloo Railway Station where they were photographed for England's Daily Express newspaper. From here, ABBA went to London's Hyde Park, where they were photographed with the Swedish Ambassador, Ole Johahl. Here, Ole formally congratulated ABBA, and told them "This is my proudest day in England. You are all fine ambassadors yourself."

Despite having a busy promotional schedule, ABBA did find some time to see the sights of London. Anni-Frid was very impressed with the clothes shops, whilst Benny sampled the pints of beer in some traditional English pubs. However, a recurring throat complaint meant that Agnetha had to spend her last day in London in bed at her hotel. On Wednesday 10th April ABBA travelled to Holland to make an appearance on a Dutch TV show.

After appearing on a German TV show on Thursday, ABBA's thoughts turned to the forthcoming Easter holidays. ABBA spent Easter on their island in Stockholm's Archipelago. For the first time in weeks, ABBA could spend time with their families and children. The past week had been the most important week of their lives – but now it was time to rest.

CHAPTER SEVEN
EUROPE SURRENDERS

ABBA emerged from the Easter holidays feeling happy and refreshed, their sense of happiness greatly enhanced by the knowledge that 'Waterloo' was a massive hit around the world. Within a few weeks 'Waterloo' had made the number one position in England, France, Germany, Holland, Denmark, Austria, Belgium, Luxembourg, Switzerland, Ireland, Norway, Finland, Sweden and Australia. In America, 'Waterloo', peaked at number six on the Billboard charts.

However, ABBA's newly-found international success was soon to cause outrage in their native country, Sweden. In January 1974 ABBA had verbally agreed to embark on a tour of Sweden's 'folk parks' during July, but in view of their Eurovision victory they needed to reorganise their schedule. Therefore, realising that the 'folk park' tour would require one month preparation and one month of performing, ABBA decided that they no longer had the time or energy to carry it through. On 16th April ABBA announced to the Swedish press that they were going to cancel the 'folk park' tour. Immediately voices of discontent were raised from all sides – the press, the promoters and the fans. Everyone thought that now ABBA had achieved their first international hit record, they were turning their backs on their own people and country. Arne Soderlund, Director of the 'folk park' entertainment section, issued the following statement – "ABBA's decision is terribly immoral. ABBA has won an important international music competition with the support of the Swedish people. Now they abandon their home audience completely to concentrate on the foreign markets".

These sentiments were shared by the 'folk park' tour organisers, with one organiser saying "This is, without question, the ugliest betrayal I have experienced in my many years in this business. I have engaged the greatest stars in the entire world and now I am ridiculed by a group of Swedish amateurs, assuredly forgotten within one year." The voices of discontent were soon damped, however, when ABBA announced that in November they would be embarking on their first tour of Eurpoe. Naturally, dates on the tour would include performances throughout Sweden, proving that ABBA were not abandoning their home audience, but just making them wait a while.

During May ABBA released their first album, titled 'ABBA Waterloo'. The album contained twelve songs: "Waterloo', 'Sitting In Your Palmtree', 'King Kong Song', Hasta Manana', 'My Mamma Said', 'Dance (While The Music Still Goes On)', 'Honey Honey', 'Watch Out', 'What About Livingstone', 'Gonna Sing You My Lovesong', 'Suzy Hangaround', and 'Ring Ring. With the release of the album during May ABBA embarked on a promotional tour which took them to France, Germany, Italy, Belgium, Holland and England.

Whilst 'ABBA – Waterloo' was steadily selling throughout Europe during the summer months, ABBA stayed in Stockholm. Benny and Bjorn continued writing new songs for ABBA and also produced two albums for fellow Polar Music artists, Lena Andersson and Ted Gargestad. Agnetha and Frida (as she was now being referred to), seized the opportunity to prepare their voices and bodies for ABBA's forthcoming European tour. As well as attending singing lessons, Agnetha and Frida were also given dance lessons by American choreographer Graham Tainton.

During the Summer, ABBA's attack on the world charts continued when their new single, 'Honey Honey' was released and provided them with a second hit single throughout Europe. However, in England it proved to be far more difficult for ABBA to score a second hit single.

On 21st June a slightly re-mixed version of 'Ring Ring' was released as a single in England. During May, ABBA had returned to England to perform 'Ring Ring' for Top fof the Pops; however, due to industrial action at the BBC, the performance was never transmitted. This lack of exposure resulted in 'Ring Ring' taking weeks and weeks to make an impression on the charts. When it finally did manage to reach the charts during July, the highest position in reached was number thirty-two. The English press were quick to report their suspiscions that ABBA were 'one-hit wonders'.

During September ABBA made their first visit to America. In August, Rolling Stone magazine had paved the way for ABBA's first American visit by publishing a very favourable article about them, written by Ken Barnes – "ABBA's emergence is one of the most cheering musical events in recent months. Just when the Top 40 was plubming hetherto unfathomable moribund depths, along came their single 'Waterloo'. A modern day 'girl group' production with the brightest, most exuberant sound around. It's made button punching on the car radio a worthwhile pastime once again. With their concise, upbeat pop creations, ABBA is much closer to the essential spirit of rock 'n' roll than any number of self-indulgent, hot-shot guitarists or devotional groups, handing down cosmic, dynamic enlightenment to the huddled masses. Anti-pop snobbery is an obselete relic of the Sixties and the time has come to abandon it – or else you will miss out on albums as perfectly delightful as 'Waterloo'."

When ABBA arrived in America they were greeted with much curiosity. At the Swedish Information Office in New York, ABBA met the American press for the first time. Here ABBA talked to numerous journalists and conducted several photo sessions. The following day, the journalists relayed their first impressions of ABBA to their magazine and newspaper readers. An article by Anthony-Heden Guest appeared in Rolling Stone magazine and questioned the value of a 'Eurovision' win. He pointed out that all previous wins had been "exhilarating but short-lived", and predicted that ABBA would be "no exception". By contrast, another article for another magazine described ABBA's 'Waterloo' album as "a positive blast of inspirational music" and said that ABBA had the potential to "make it big". The article ended by telling its readers "Watch out for another supergroup".

"A positive blast of inspirational music."

Before leaving America ABBA travelled to Philadelphia, where they appeared on the highly rated 'Mike Douglas Show'. Although the 'Waterloo' album failed to reach further than 150 on the American charts, the fact that the single 'Waterloo' had reached number six, and ABBA's latest American release, 'Honey Honey', was making a big impression on the charts, proved to be a very encouraging sign for ABBA.

CHAPTER EIGHT
STOP-LOOK-and LISTEN

ABBA viewed their first European Tour as an ideal oppportunity to present themselves in person to their increasing army of European fans. With the eyes and ears of their fans and critics upon them, ABBA needed to reproduce a sound equal to their records and an image that was as dramatic as their performance at the Eurovision Song Contest. Therefore, in order to achieve these results, ABBA employed the services of highly-skilled friends and acquaintances. Thomas Johansson and Knud Thorbjornsen had been employed to arrange the tour, and during the summer they had ensured that all preparations were in order for ABBA's debut concert. Bjorn's ex-Hootenanny Singers friend, Hansi Schwartz, was employed as tour leader, whilst the popular Swedish dance band, The Beatmakers, were ABBA's guest musicians. ABBA's sound was managed by their studio engineer, Michael B Tretow, together with Calbbe af Geijerstam (one half of Malta Duo, who beat ABBA in the 1973 Swedish heats of the Eurovision Song Contest). For their all-important job, Michael and Clabbe enlisted the help of twenty-eight speaker units, fifteen mixing desks, eighteen stereo phasers and a control unit, comprising of forty separate buttons and levers.

As for the visual aspect of the tour, this was left up to ABBA themselves. With Agnetha's skin-tight suit, Frida's glittery mini skirt, Bjorn's equally glittery trousers and Benny's eye-catching leopard design jacket, there would be no shortage of colourful and sometimes outrageous costume changes. The tour was broken up into three stages. In each stage, ABBA would perform for two weeks, and then return to Sweden for a break so that Agnetha and Bjorn could be with their young daughter. After spending the whole of October rehearsing, ABBA were ready to face their audience.

Before a sell-out audience, on Sunday 17th November 1974, ABBA gave a preview of their show at Falkonerteater, Copenhagen, Denmark. Included in the audience were Europe's music critics and journalists, all eager to report upon ABBA's debut performance.
"A glittering show in both clothes and colour, with good choreography, fine sound balance, and surprisingly catchy new tunes in the repertoire", wrote Hans Fridlund for Expressen, whilst Erik Ahman, for Gothegorgs Posten, described ABBA's performance as "A show that had everything, tempo, rhythm and tunes that stuck in your head." Tore Ljungberg, for Arbetet, wrote "A blazing, high tempo and well directed rock show."
Inevitably, there were negative reviews; however, they were not so much for ABBA's performance as for the noise level of the show. "The sound level was far too high for a family show" and "The charming women fought a helpless battle against amplifiers and kilowatts" reported two newspapers.

For the next thirteen days ABBA took their show to West Germany, (Hanover, Munich, Frankfurt, Berlin, Nuemburg, Dusseldorf, Bremen and Hamburg), and then on to Austria and Switzerland. After one week's rest, on 8th December, stage two of the tour commenced. Initially this stage of the tour was to take ABBA to England for five shows; however, two factors prevented ABBA from going. Firstly, ABBA were still fighting hard to be taken seriously in England, and secondly, the cost of transporting all the equipment to England was far too expensive to justify.

The decision to leave out England meant that ABBA could begin their Christmas holidays early. For Benny and Bjorn it meant that they had more time to write new material for ABBA. Up until now, ABBA's European Tour had not been the success that they had hoped for. Except for the first show in Copenhagen, none of the other shows were sell-outs, resulting in ABBA's losing a vast amount of money. One further thing that had surprised ABBA was the age of their audience. The average age of each audience was between twenty-five and forty. With the age of the audience being much higher than they had anticipated, ABBA found arousing enthusiasm at their shows very difficult. However, when ABBA commenced the third and final stage of their tour, on 10th January 1975, the tables were completely turned. This stage took ABBA through Norway and Sweden. Their first show at the Chateau Nuef, Oslo, Norway, was a complete sell-out, as were all the remaining shows. At one show at the Scandanavium in Gothenburg, seven thousand fans came to see ABBA, with thousands more being turned away for not having tickets. In Stockholm there was more hysteria, which led promoter, Sid Bernstein, to delcare ABBA "The Swedish Beatles". As the tour ended in Umea, Northern Sweden on 22nd January, ABBA left their Scandanavian audiences wanting more. For this, they would have to wait until June, when ABBA would commence a short tour of Sweden's 'folk parks'. In the meantime ABBA concentrated on recording their second album, which they hoped would extend their success in Scandanavia to countries around the world.

ABBA

While ABBA were preoccupied with their tour during November 1974, they released a new single in Europe called 'So Long'. Throughout Europe, 'So Long' gave ABBA a second hit single and it achieved high chart positions in France, Germany, Holland, Denmark, Sweden, Austria and Switerland. However, in the country where it really mattered, England, 'So Long' failed to make any impression at all. Despite being back at 'square one' as far as the English market was concerned, ABBA remained optimistic and channelled all their energy into completing their second album.

During the first four months of 1975, ABBA recorded their new album at Glestudio and Metronome Studios in Stockholm. Once all the vocals had been recorded, Agnetha and Frida left Benny and Bjorn to produce, mix and arrange the album, while they recorded their own solo albums for the Swedish market. Agnetha chose Glenstudio to record her sixth and final Swedish solo album, titled 'Elva Kninnor I Ett Hus' (Eleven Women In One House'). Together with Bosse Carlgren, Agnetha had written all the songs on her album, with the exception of a song titled 'SOS', which Benny and Bjorn had written especially for her. The recording of the album presented Agnetha with a totally new experience, for she also produced the album. "It was great fun to watch over a thing and build it up by myself. To be able to sit and mix and see the results develop is wonderful" she said.
Frida recorded her solo album at Metronome Studios, and Benny took time off from working with ABBA material to produce the album for her. Titled 'Ensam' ('Alone'), for her album Frida mixed old, well-known songs with new. Her interpretations of 'Life on Mars', 'Wall Street Shuffle', 'The Most Beautiful Girl', 'Send In The Clowns', 'Wouldn't It Be Nice' and 'Young Girl' provided the old, whilst 'Fernando', a song specially written for Frida by Benny and Bjorn, provided the new.

By May ABBA's second album was ready to be released. Titled 'ABBA', the album contained eleven songs: 'Mamma Mia', 'Hey Hey Helen', 'Tropical Loveland', 'SOS', 'Man In The Middle', 'Bang A Boomerang', 'I Do I Do I Do I Do I Do', 'Rock Me', 'Intermezzo No. 1', 'I've Been Waiting For You' and 'So Long'. ABBA was released in Sweden first, where advance orders exeeded 150,000 copies. Both commercially and critically, 'ABBA' was an immediate success. "ABBA have polished their style and have become more daring. There are no weak songs here. Bjorn and Berry can now produce sharp, easy to remember tunes, with the ease of scratching one's head", wrote Mats Olsson for Expressen, whilst Leif J. Andersson, for Goteborgs Posten, wrote "It is typical ABBA, straight, sharp songs, with the strength to keep them in your memory". Christer Borg, for Kvallposten, wrote "This album is yet another confirmation that 'Waterloo' was not just a brilliant exception. This is quite simply an unusally professional product". The only negative criticism directed at ABBA's latest album appeared in Aftonbladet. It read "The lyrics and musical orginality disappear in this electronic and lifeless stew. All personality is lost and it is sad to see such musical talent sell itself so royally. All that is left are four jerking plastic dolls."

However, these last comments did not deter one in every twenty Swedes from buying the album and pushing its sales past 400,000 copies – a figure never before achieved by anyone in Sweden. Before the album was released worldwide, ABBA released a new single taken from the album, titled 'I Do I Do I Do I Do I Do'. Throughout Europe 'I Do I Do I Do I Do I Do' was an immediate hit, except in England. The English music critics dismissed the single as soon as it was released. "This song is so bad – it hurts. We can all do without it" wrote Melody Maker.

Ironically, when 'ABBA' was released worldwide during June it was the same Melody Maker magazine that gave ABBA's latest album one of the more encouraging reviews, by saying "This is an interesting album with good tunes and good, strong musicianship." Going even further, another English critic wrote "ABBA are a group who bring a startling professionalism and integrity to their work that's worth anybody's time and money." Harry Doherty's review for Disc magazine was less complimentary, saying "ABBA, poor ABBA, had so many good intentions with this album. This album contains a few tracks that would make exceptionally good singles, but the other material isn't worth mentioning. Stick to singles ABBA, you are just a mediocre album band."

Throughout Europe, where ABBA had already gained widespread popularity with their single releases, 'ABBA' was an immediate hit, and firmly cemented ABBA's popularity. It was during this time that ABBA's popularity started to soar in two territories that up until now had taken a back seat – Australia and Eastern Europe.

In June 1975, Edward Gierek, a leading politicain from Poland, made an official visit to Sweden. Being the first offical visit of its kind, the media coverage both in Poland and Sweden was great. To coincide with the visit, Polish newspapers published large colour supplements that covered every aspect of Swedish life. In one particular supplement that dealt with Sweden's music scene, a large colour photograph of ABBA was printed, together with their fan club address in Stockholm. Within weeks of the article being published, ABBA's fan club received sacks full of letters from Polish fans. In the first few sacks alone there were more than ten thousand letters.

This mass interest in ABBA from Eastern Europe took everyone by surprise, but, at the same time, could not be ignored. Therefore, Stig immediately began to make plans for ABBA's records to be released in Poland. Throughout Eastern Europe, all the record companies were owned by the governments and, in turn, each record company only received a limited budget each year for the purpose of importing 'Western music'. Once that budget was spent, the record companies would have to wait until the following year before receiving further funds from their government. Such was ABBA's popularity throughout Poland that its record company decided to spend its entire budget on ABBA records. When ABBA's album 'ABBA' was released 250,000 copies were immediately sold in Poland – a figure that could easily have been quadrupled, said the record company. In Russia, an unknown territory as far as 'Western Music' was concerned, permission was granted for 25,000 ABBA records to be released. ABBA's increasing popularity throughout Eastern Europe resulted in the demand for their records far exceeding their availability. As a consequence of these music 'restrictions', ABBA records were beginning to sell for vast amounts of money on the 'black market' in Eastern Europe.

Meanwhile, the impact ABBA were making throughout Australia was generating interest never before seen in that country. Already, six ABBA singles had been released in Australia – 'Waterloo', 'Ring Ring', 'Honey Honey', 'So Long', 'I've Been Waiting For You' and 'I Do I Do I Do I Do I Do', all had made an enormous impression on the Australian charts. However, it was not until the Australian television programme 'Countdown' screened a short clip of ABBA's video for 'Mamma Mia' that the population of Australia really stood up and took notice. The public response to the video clip was so overwhelming that ABBA's Austrialian record company. RCA immediately contacted Polar Music for permission to release 'Mamma Mia' as a single. Initially Polar Music denied them permission, for fear of ABBA being 'over exploited' in Australia. However, after consideration and several later requests, Polar Music agreed to release 'Mamma Mia', as a single in Australia. ABBA knew that 'Mamma Mia' was a strong song and had the potential to be a single release. Therefore, by allowing it to be released in Australia first, they could see exactly if 'Mamma Mia' could actually stand up by itself. When released, 'Mamma Mia' immediately topped the Australian charts and remained at the top for several weeks. Within weeks, 'Mamma Mia' was declared Australia's biggest selling single in chart history, a feat that remains to this day. Never before had a pop group generated so much interest in Australia, and 'ABBAMANIA' was declared.

Back in Sweden 'ABBAMANIA' was also gripping the country as ABBA embarked on a fourteen day tour of Sweden's 'folk parks'. From their first concert in Skelleftea on 24th June to their last, in Gamleby on 9th July, over 100,000 fans went to see ABBA. At the concert in Gronalund in Stockholm, ABBA were greeted by 19,000 fans, and scenes of mass hysteria followed them everywhere. However, the tour was nearly brought to an abrupt end when Agnetha's recurring throat problem once again reared its ugly head. The night before ABBA were due to perform in Malmo, Agnetha was taken ill and had a temperature of forty degrees. "That night in Malmo was a nightmare" recalled Agnetha. "Ten minutes before we were due to perform, my legs shook and I sat and cried. Somehow I managed to get through the show, but we had our doctor, Ake Olsson, behind the scenes, just in case something happened." Agnetha's illness resulted in two shows in Kinloping and Gamleby having to be postponed, but the following week ABBA returned to honour their commitment.

Because of the great success of the 'folk park' tour, ABBA finally managed to recoup the money that they had invested in their less successful European Tour. After negotiations with the 'folk park' organisers, ABBA were paid sixty per cent of the ticket sales, meaning that they now had 250,000 Crowns to share between them.

During the summer of 1975 ABBA rested and refected upon the past twelve months of travelling, touring and recording. During those twelve months ABBA had slowly but surely been accepted by their European audience, invited into the 'closed' world of Eastern Europe had been declared 'superstars' in Sweden and Australia. All that was needed now was acceptance and recognition from the two most influential markets – England and America.

"Ten minutes before we were due to perform, my legs shook and I sat and cried."

CHAPTER NINE
SENDING OUT AN SOS

Sufficiently satisfied with the progress that they had made throughout Europe and Australia, ABBA now turned their attention to England and America. For any hope of achieving true international recognition, these two makrets needed to be broken. First came 'Waterloo', and then came very little. Despite 'Ring Ring', 'Honey Honey', 'So Long' and 'I Do I Do I Do I Do I Do' becoming minor successes in America, there was still a lot of work needing to be done. England, however, just did not want to know. How could a pop group from Sweden expect to be taken seriously? Furthermore, how could a winner of the Eurovision Song Contest have any chance of continued success? It was attitudes like this that greatly hindered ABBA's attempt to break the English market. However, looking at the situation positively, it was attitudes like that that made ABBA even more determined to succeed. With their next single release, ABBA needed to prove to their audience and critics that they had the ability to expand their musical talents. The song that best met these requirements, as far as ABBA were concerned, was 'SOS'. "We though that 'SOS' would make a very good single and at the same time would give our fans some sort of clue as to what musical direction we heading for. That in itself would have meant as much to us as having a number one" said Bjorn.

During August 'SOS' was released throughout Europe, followed by a September release in England and America. Immediately 'SOS' took the world charts by storm, and within weeks, was a number one in Germany, Holland, Denmark, Finland, Sweden, Australia, South Africa, and New Zealand. In France it reached the number two position and in Switzerland number three. However, perhaps more importantly, it was 'SOS' that ended eighteen months of uncertainty as far as England was concerned. After making an immediate impact on the English charts, 'SOS' finally peaked at number six. In America 'SOS' gave ABBA their biggest hit to date by reaching number ten on the Billboard charts. After months and months of uncertainty, ABBA had now proved to their English and American audience that they were indeed a force to be reckoned with.

While 'SOS' made its mark on the world charts, ABBA spent the whole of September in the television studios in Stockholm, rehearsing and recording their first TV Special. Called 'ABBA – Made In Sweden, for Export', the sixty-minute special was primarily aimed at the European and Australian markets. ABBA saw their first TV Special as an ideal opportunity to present themselves to their fans, via television, in many countries at the same time, without the inconvenience of travelling. It also provided their fans with a unique chance to see ABBA, performing, live on stage, their hit records to date: 'Waterloo', 'Ring Ring', 'Honey Honey', 'So Long', 'I Do I Do I Do I Do I Do' and 'SOS'.

Following an invitation from Michael B. Tretow (ABBA's studio engineer and close friend), October saw Agnetha, Benny, Bjorn and Frida at Glenstudio, Stockholm, where they helped Michael with the recording of his own album, titled 'Let's Boogie'. For the next four months, in between their ABBA commitments, Agnetha and Frida sang backing vocals, and Benny and Bjorn played keyboards and guitar on eleven of the album's twelve songs –

'Paper Dolls', 'Robot Man', 'Bottom Coming Up', 'Brief Intermission', 'Moonbeams', 'I Can See What You Mean', 'That's The Way The Cookie Crumbles', 'Sandwich', 'Hesitating Hanna', 'Keep Your Hands To Yourself', 'Doc Mc Gurgle's Babylonian Lizard Tooth Oil', and 'He Can't Sing'. When completed, two things stood out from the album. Firstly, the production of 'Let's Boogie' was technically very advanced and secondly, Agnetha and Frida's unmistakable vocals. "I've tried everything that I haven't been able to get Benny and Bjorn to try. I have come up with a whole lot of groovy sounds that might find a place on ABBA's records in the future" said Michael.

During November ABBA travelled to America for a two-week promotional visit. Since their first visit to America in September 1974, ABBA had gained much ground in terms of success and popularity, as highlighted in an article in America's Cashbox magazine by Phil Alexandar –

which greeted ABBA upon their arrival in America. Titled "International Hitmakers ABBA", the article read, "Not in recent memory – perhaps not since the emergence of The Beatles – has anyone so completely captured the attention of music people and music consumers. One may say that they have an excellent chance of happening here in a very big way. Those singles from this year's album, "ABBA", are definitive examples of the powerful, well-constructed ability ABBA has for reaching that nebulous level of musical comprehension that exists on the part of music listeners wordwide. One of the most expertly engineered and mixed collaborations of its genre."

Beginning in San Diego, on the Mike Douglas show, ABBA went on to appear on a further six television shows throughout America. Next was Las Vagas where ABBA appeared on the Merv Griffin Show from Caesar's Palace. Here ABBA were introduced as "An international supermusic group" by their friend, Neil Sedaka. From here ABBA travelled to Los Angeles, where they appeared on 'American Bandstand', 'Music Thing', 'Don Kirshner's Rock Concert' and 'The Dinah Shore Show'. It was on 'The Dinah Shore Show' that Benny and Frida were made an offer that took them totally by surprise: "I understand that you two have been too busy to get married" said Dinah, "Well . . . if you would like to marry here and now, you can, in front of millions of American television viewers." A surprised Benny and Frida politely declined the offer, saying "We will get married when we have the time and in a place we want to".

ABBA concluded their visit to America in New York. Here ABBA appeared on the live 'Saturday Night Show', together with the 'guest artist of the week', Paul Simon. ABBA opened the show with their current American hit, 'SOS', and closed the show with 'Waterloo'. Before leaving America ABBA were presented with two awards. Firstly, the American composers' organisation, 'BMI', voted "SOS' one of the most popular songs of 1975 in America. This was proved by the second award – a gold disc for 'SOS', after it had achieved over one million sales in America.

Back home in Sweden, Benny and Bjorn took some time away from ABBA commitments in order to produce an album for fellow Polar artist Ted Gardestad. On the other hand, Agnetha and Frida released their solo albums 'Elva Kvinnor I Ett Hus' and 'Ensam'. However, not wanting to jeopardise the image of 'ABBA the group', Stig insisted that Agnetha and Frida should not perform their solo material on television, but despite this both albums did very well.

Frida's album 'Ensam' was an immediate hit and was critically acclaimed by fans and critics alike. With total sales exceeding 100,000 copies, Frida was guaranteed number one position on the Swedish charts.

Agnetha's 'Elva Kvinnor I Ett Hus' was less successful, after both Agnetha and her album were given a tough time by the critcs. "Next time get rid of those ridiculous lyrics . . .

"Not in recent memory – perhaps not since the emergence of The Beatles – has anyone so completely captured the attention of music people and music consumers."

. . . I want to know Agnetha more that I want to know about a lot of made up people who live in a house that doesn't exist" wrote Mats Olsson. Even Agentha's appearance came in for criticism. For many years Agnetha had had a gap between her front teeth. This gap had now naturally closed up, but people began to say that, in an attempt to make herself more beautiful, Agnetha had had an operation on her teeth. These reports not only hurt Angetha, but angered her. "Why do people have to say things like this? I have not received any treatment on my teeth since I was eleven years old" she said.

Following the success of 'SOS', November saw ABBA release their follow up single, 'Mamma Mia', throughout Europe. Already a massive hit in Australia, it was now time for 'Mamma Mia' to prove itself everywhere else. Released first in England on 14th November, 'Mamma Mia' made an immediate impact on the English charts. Elsewhere throughout Europe 'Mamma Mian' was released during December, and it was not long before ABBA scored another hit single.

With 'Mamma Mia' ending the year riding high on Europe's charts, ABBA could happily look forward to their Christmas holidays, which presented Benny and Bjorn with the ideal opportunity to add the final touches to a couple of new ABBA songs. For Agnetha the Christmas holidays presented an opportunity to go to hospital and have her tonsils removed.

As the Christmas festivities began, ABBA could happy reflect upon a busy but successful year that had taken them to new heights. At last it seemed that everything was going their way.

CHAPTER TEN
THE ARRIVAL OF ABBA

ABBA could not have wished for a better start to 1976. As they emerged from the Christmas holidays, they soon learned that 'Mamma Mia' was number one in many countries, including France, Germany, Holland, Denmark, Austria, Finland, Luxembourg, Belgium, Switzerland, Israel and The West Indies. But the best news was still to come. During the third week of January, 'Mamma Mia' reached the number one position in England, after Queen's 'Bohemian Rhapsody' ended a nine-week reign at the top of England's charts. ABBA immediately visited England to record 'Mamma Mia' for Top Of The Pops. They again met the English press, who could no longer describe ABBA as a 'one hit wonder'. During their many press interviews Benny and Bjorn made some strong points regarding England's 'negative' and 'narrow-minded' attitude to ABBA and their music:

BJORN – "This is the first time we've come to England since Eurovision and have been met with some sort of respect. Now people believe that we're not just a one-hit group, and that we're something that's going to continue and do a lot more"

BENNY – "In England we didn't get the image we deserved. Because we won Eurovision, we got the image that goes with Eurovision, and it's not really correct. We just happened to be in the contest. For example, I think we'd prefer the sort of image The Mammas and the Pappas had. The thing is that England has been a most difficult market for us. We've had hits in Europe, Australia and America, but England has been reluctant. But we never thought "let's forget it". We thought that it was extremeley difficult to reach the English, but we believe so much in ourselves, we have so much self-confidence, that we agreed that sooner or later it was bound to happen in England. Fortunately, we have been proved right".

Benny and Bjorn also relealed to the press that ABBA wished to be recognised as an albums band, and not just a singles band.

BENNY – "The singles aren't really representative of everything we do. What we wish is that we could become an albums band – our albums have a lot more to give than just a single. We agree that we write quite simple songs, but they are catchy and there is a lot of effort put into the arrangements. The only thing that gets exposure is a single, and normally a group like us doesn't make good albums and that's what probably frightens people off. But we go in and try to record ten very good singles for an album, and people don't notice that. It is not really important for us to have a number one single. What is important is that people sit and listen to the music that we play and like what they hear".

For the majority of January and February ABBA were at Metronome Studios, Stockholm, where they recorded some new songs for their next album. During March ABBA released their new single, titled 'Fernando', worldwide. Already 'Fernando' had been a huge solo hit for Frida in Sweden, where it was released as the single from her 'Ensam' album. This success had inspired Benny, Bjorn and Stig to re-record the song with English lyrics and release it as an offical ABBA song. However, ABBA were unable to wait and see what the world's reaction would be to their new single as they were travelling, for a seven-day visit to Australia, the country where 'ABBAMANIA' was spreading like wildfire.

As reported previously by the Australian press, ABBA were "The biggest thing to hit Australia since Tornado Tracey"; therefore, when ABBA arrived at Melbourne Airport for their first-ever visit to Australia, thousands of fans had turned out to greet them. "As we stepped off the plane in Melbourne, I looked at Frida. She had tears in her eyes – just as I had. We were so moved by the reception awaiting us" recalled Agnetha. ABBA's first few days in Australia were spent in Melbourne, where they held a press conference and conducted numerous television, radio and press interviews, as well as many photo sessions. From here ABBA travelled to Sydney. In Sydney the scenes of mass hysteria were equal to those witnessed in Melbourne, and when asked by a journalist "What are your first impressions of Australia?", ABBA were unanimous in saying "It is a great pleasure for us to be here. The Australian people are quite fantastic – they are all so warm and friendly."

The highlight of ABBA's first visit to Australia was a forty-five minute TV Special recorded for Channel 9 in Sydney. Before a live audience, ABBA performed a string of their hit singles, 'Waterloo', 'Ring Ring', 'SOS', 'Mamma Mia', 'Rock Me' and 'Fernando'. ABBA were also filmed at Sydney Zoo and walking along Sydney beach the previous day. When Channel 9 screened their 'ABBA TV Special', further evidence of ABBA's phenomenal popularity in Australia was plain to see; an amazing 58% of the Australian population tuned in to watch ABBA. Never before in Australian television history had so many people watched the same programme, and Channel 9 had to repeat the TV Special in order to satisfy the overwhelming public demand.

Whilst ABBA were taking Australia by storm, Stig and Thomas Johansson (ABBA's tour organiser) were viewing Australia's best concert arenas in order to see which ones would best accommodate ABBA in 1977, whey they would return to Australia for their first concert tour. With the Australian public eagerly awaiting their return ABBA travelled back to Sweden leaving no fewer than five of their songs riding high on the Australian charts – 'Fernando' was at number one, 'Ring Ring' at number four, 'Rock Me' at number five, 'Mamma Mia' at twenty and 'SOS' at twenty-two.

Upon their return to Sweden, ABBA soon learned of 'Fernando's' worldwide success. Already 'Fernando' had reached the number one position in England, Holland, Denmark, Germany, Sweden, Finland, Austria, Switzerland, Israel, Luxembourg, France, New Zealand and The West Indies.

"The Australian people are quite fantastic – they are all so warm and friendly."

During the last week of March ABBA's attack on the world charts continued when they released a 'Greatest Hits' album. "ABBA – Greatest Hits Vol 1" contained fifteen of their most successful and best known songs: 'SOS', 'He Is Your Brother', 'Ring Ring', 'Hasta Manana', 'Nina Pretty Ballerina', 'Honey Honey', 'So Long', 'I Do I Do I Do I Do I Do', 'People Need Love', 'Bang A Boomerang', 'Another Town Another Train', 'Dance (While The Music Still Goes On)'. 'Waterloo' and 'Fernando'. 'Greatest Hits' was an immediate success and put ABBA at number one on both the album and single charts in very many countries.

In England 'Greatest Hits' was one of the very first albums to be advertised on television, and advance orders exceeding 100,000 copies were placed. Within four weeks of its release, 'Greatest Hits' was at number one in England, where it remained for nine weeks. During April, May and June, ABBA were at Metronome Studios, where they worked solidly on their forthcoming new album. On the 18th June ABBA came out of hiding for one day only.

The weekend of Friday 18th June was one of celebration throughout Sweden, for King Carl Gustaf was to marry Miss Silvia Sommerlath, and so Sweden would have a new Queen. On the even of the 'Royal Wedding' a spectacular musical gala was presented to the 'Royal Couple' at Stockholm's Royal Opera House. At the gala, ABBA were the only pop musicians invited to perform, the remaining artists being of 'classical' background. When ABBA stepped on stage, dressed in regal outfits to fit the occasion, they provided the 'Royal Couple', audience and television viewers with an exclusive performance of a new ABBA song, titled 'Dancing Queen'. Immediately, the Swedish people assumed that Benny and Bjorn must have written the song for their new Queen. However, this was not true. "'Dancing Queen' has in fact been written for six months, but the title was just perfect for the occasion so we used it. We think it is a nice tribute to our new Queen, but a lot of people have got the wrong idea about it" said Bjorn.

Despite Bjorn's statement the Swedish people still thought of 'Dancing Queen' as the 'Royal Wedding song', and there was great public demand for ABBA to release it as a single immediately. ABBA did not want to release a new single until their new album was complete, but public pressure forced them to re-schedule their plans. As preparations were made to release 'Dancing Queen' as ABBA's new single sooner rather than later, ABBA spent the remainder of June and July recording their new album.

On 6th August 'Dancing Queen' was released as the new ABBA single. Its impact on the world charts was phenomenal; as fans and critics agreed, 'Dancing Queen' was ABBA's best song to date. "'Dancing Queen' is surely the most advanced production ABBA has done – it is a little disco in rhythm. but all the rest of it, all the small bits – the chattering piano, the singing girls – it begins to be more and more typical of ABBA. Bjorn and Benny have studied the studio – and mastered it" wrote Mats Olsson for Expressen.

'Dancing Queen' was an immediate hit throughout the world, and before August came to an end it was a number one in fifteen different countries. In England 500,000 copies of 'Dancing Queen' were sold, and guaranteed ABBA their third consecutive number one single. It was during August that Sweden, and in particular Swedish Television, began to realise to true extent of ABBA's international success and popularity. Therefore Swedish Television decided to pay tribute to ABBA and began filming their first ABBA TV Special. ABBA had just completed their new album and so, during August and September, they turned their attention to filming.

Titled 'ABBA D'ABBA DOO' and produced by Leonard Eek, ABBA were filmed at work and at play in various locations, including on their 'secret' island in Stockholm's Archipelago. Per Falkman also conducted a series of interviews with ABBA in which they talked about their childhoods and their hard fight to be accepted and recognised by thei native Sweden. ABBA also talked about how their music is of utmost importance and not the fan adoration and press speculation that surrounds an international pop group.

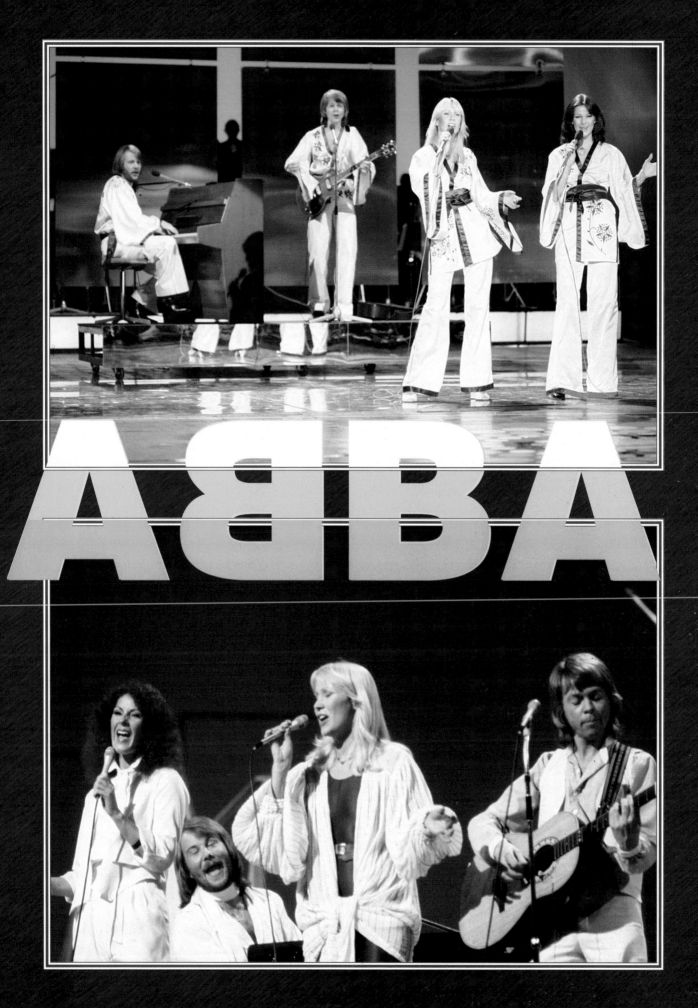

ABBA

In September ABBA were filmed performing nine songs from their forthcoming album before a live audience in Stockholm. When completed at the end of September, "ABBA D'ABBA DOO' showed ABBA as they really were, four normal down-to-earth Swedes with very big talents, who had achieved worldwide success and popularity through their music. Although 'ABBA D'ABBA DOO' was a product of Swedish Television, aimed primarily at the Swedish market, many other countries, including England, Australia and Germany, had expressed a great interest in buying the programme. Therefore, for international purposes, 'ABBA D'ABBA DOO' was re-recorded with English dialogue, and re-named 'ABBA From the Beginning'.

During October ABBA visited Poland for the first time. Already ABBA were generating huge interest there and were hailed as "The most popular group in Eastern Europe". Because of ABBA's unique acceptance in Eastern Europe, the Polish Government did everything they could to make them feel welcome. As ABBA arrived at Warsaw Airport, in a private plane courtesy of the Polish Authorities, over two hundred journalists and photographers were there to greet them. At the airport ABBA held a press conference at which they were interviewed and photographed by press representatives from Poland, Russia and East Germany.

After the press conference ABBA were taken to the televison studios in Warsaw, where they recorded a TV Special for Poland. 'Studio 2' was Poland's monthly entertainment programme, hosted by National celebrities Edward Mikolajczyk and Bozena Walter. This month ABBA dominated the programme as they performed eight songs, five of them being from their forthcoming album. Before leaving Poland, ABBA were presented with an array of gold and silver awards for the vast sales of their records in Poland.

On Sunday 10th October, ABBA travelled to America for their third promotional visit. ABBA were making steady progress throughout America, as highlighted in two articles from Billboard and Cashbox magazines prior to their current visit. Billboard said "Some may regard ABBA's sweet, sparkling, highly-commercial pop-rock sound as lightweight, but the group was hip enough this season to get a guest spot on 'Saturday Night'. And it does put together consistently entertaining singles that sell around the world. The Scandinavian outfit have racked up five Top 40 hits in the US." Cashbox went further, by saying "When it comes to pop music, many European groups have always displayed an uncanny understanding of this essential musical form – and ABBA is certainly one of them. ABBA is the perfect example of what European pop music is all about – the vocals are clean and instantly dominant, the melodies catchy and generously spiced with good, pop hooks."

Arriving in America, ABBA were faced with three weeks of interviews, television shows and travelling that would also take them to Canada for the first time. In total, ABBA made appearances on seven television shows – 'The Dinah Shore Show', 'The Mike Douglas Show', two 'Midnight Specials' shows, 'Don Kirschner's Rock Concert' and two Canadian TV shows. One highlight of ABBA's visit to America came when British singer/actor Anthony Newley presented ABBA with an award from England's The Sun Newspaper. ABBA had been voted the most popular entertainers to appear on British TV during 1976.

ABBA's third visit to America had been a huge success, and paved the way for their latest American single release, 'Dancing Queen'. Before leaving, Bjorn said "If 'Dancing Queen' becomes a hit, we would be willing to return to America. We are interested in doing concerts in four or five big, important American cities, but when – it's impossible to say at the moment".

When 'Dancing Queen' was released in America and Canda, it was received very well by the critics. Billboard magazine said "The good-timey Swedish group that makes the Top Twenty with just about every single, returns to its almost characteristic novelty groove. Although the melody is ABBA at its bounciest, the lyrics have considerable substance dealing with a youthful peak experience of being belle of the disco ball at seventeen. The sweep of the vocal harmonies almost recall the heyday of The Mammas and The Papas", whilst Cashbox said "Following a Top Ten success with 'Fernando', the international scene's masters of pop music have come up with a song, backed by a strong upbeat, in keeping with the title. The hooks, brought by lush and vocal harmonies, as well as the reverbsoaked wall of sound that distinguishes this group, are present. Major Top 40 adds, and the singles chart is imminent". After making an immediate impact on the American charts, 'Dancing Queen' eventually peaked at number one, giving ABBA their very first American number one single.

On Friday 5th November ABBA released their new album, titled 'Arrival', simultaneously in thirty-four different countries. The album contained ten new songs: 'When I Kissed The Teacher', 'Dancing Queen', 'My Love My Life', 'Dum Dum Diddle', 'Knowing Me Knowing You', 'Money Money Money', 'That's Me', 'Why Did It Have To Be Me?', 'Tiger' and 'Arrival'. Worldwide interest in 'Arrival' was phenonmenal, with advance orders exceeding five million pounds. Throughout Scandanavia advance orders totalled a record 750,000 copies. In England, with orders exceeding 400,000 copies, 'Arrival' set a new record for 'highest advance orders'. Up until now, Elton John's 1975 album had held the record with advance orders totally 250,000 copies.

As far as ABBA were concerned, 'Arrival' was their best album to date, as revealed by Benny, "It's the album we've spent most time and energy on, and I hope that you can tell that. I think 'Arrival' is definitely different from all the other records we have made. Personally, I mean it's the best album we've made up until now, but it hasn't been easy and that's the reason why the album is six months late – but we prefer that instead of releasing a half-finished record. You have to make yourself happy before you can make other people appreciate it. Each song on an album should be strong enough to stand up on its own".

"The vocals are clean and instantly dominant, the melodies catchy and generously spiced with good, pop hooks."

For the first time it seemed that the critics were in agreement with ABBA:

"ABBA have made their best production yet. 'Arrival' is thorough, professional and well made. ABBA occupies a special place in hit pop" wrote Mats Olsson for Expressen. "Arrival is yet another proof that Bjorn and Benny's unique ability to write internationally strong hits. Technically, the album is fully comparable to any foreign pop album. Together with technician Michael B Tretow, Bjorn and Benny have not left a single idea untested", wrote Christer Borg for Kvallsposten. Sivert Bramstedt's review for Dagens Nyheter concluded by saying "'Arrival' is a lush and effective escape from reality, to which ABBA invites us".

A69A

In England the extent of ABBA's popularity was plain to see with the release of 'Arrival'. For the first time England's music press could not dismiss ABBA and their music. Instead the leading music journals reviewed 'Arrival' in a deep and penetrating way:-

N.M.E. – "ABBA's songs are structured as surely as a Timex, they might be dismantled – but would only function again if put back together in the same way. 'Arrival' matches expectations and is their most accomplished set to date. As usual, one can only marvel at the niceties of the production. Though their instrumentation is often comparatively slight, they always achieve a full sound. ABBA are irrepressible. They deliver their material wish such gusto that if you try to turn a deaf ear, they'll just pummel your brain into submission. The band have not only patented their own style, but also shown themselves willing to introduce variations on it".

With the release of 'Arrival', ABBA embarked on a series of promotional visits to many European capitals. Once again, a busy but effective promotional campaign had been devised for ABBA, beginning in Sweden on the day of 'Arrival's release. At 8pm on Friday 5th November the whole of Sweden came to a virtual standstill when Channel 2 premiered their hour-long ABBA TV Special, 'ABBA D'ABBA DOO'. It was Sweden's television event of the year. Cafés and restaurants were converted into large television rooms. Cinemas changed their viewing times to 9pm so that people could see the ABBA TV Special. In total, more than half of Sweden's population watched 'ABBA D'ABBA DOO'.

On Monday 11th November ABBA released 'Money Money Money' as their new single. Described as "patent rubbish" by England's N.M.E. magazine, many critics felt that ABBA had chosen the wrong single to release. Many would have preferred 'Tiger' or 'That's Me'. Nevertheless, regardless of what the critics thought, 'Money Money Money' was an immediate hi around the world, reaching number one in Germany, Holland, Luxembourg, Austria, New Zealand and Australia; number two in Norway, Finland, Denmark, Switzerland and Israel; and number three in England. The B-side to 'Money Money Money' brought to light a new, never before released ABBA song titled 'Crazy World'. With lead vocals by Bjorn, the simplicity of the production indicated that 'Crazy World' had been recorded early in ABBAs career.

On Friday 15th November, ABBA arrived in England for a four-day promotional visit. After arriving at Heathrow Airport on Friday morning. ABBA's first appointment was a celebratory lunch and press conference, which had been arranged on a boat. 'Mayflower Queen', anchored on the River Thames, London.

In keeping with the sleeve design of 'Arrival', a private helicopter, complete with ABBA logo, was waiting at Heathrow Airport to ferry ABBA across London to their lunch and press conference. But the fog that had engulfed London that morning meant that ABBA's grand arrival would be somewhat later than the scheduled eleven o'clock. When ABBA finally did arrive, the army of journalists and photographers greeted them with much enthusiasm. On board the 'Mayflower Queen', ABBA drank champagne and talked to the press, but not before they had been presented with thirty-two platinum, gold and silver disc awards for their record sales in England by Radio One DJ Simon Bates. ABBA's short but amazing track record in England now spoke for itself, and Bjorn said "It is a continuing source of pleasure to us when we get these awards in Britain. Everywhere in the world, Britain is looked upon as the home of modern pop music, particularly in relation to groups."

"For were The Beatles not the first of the great world ranging groups? In fact, it was The Beatles and the song writing of Paul McCartney and John Lennon which encouraged Benny and I start writing pop songs when we did. We thought if they can do it, then so can we". Acting as spokesman, Bjorn also went on to talk about a whole range of subject relating to ABBA. He began by saying "Our feeling is that it is the music that we are making that has resulted in all these fantastic recore sales, but is's rather frightening for us to think about at times. Until the Eurovision Song Contest, two and a half years ago, the group was only really known in Sweden, although obviously we were also aiming our music at the European audiences. I guess if we had been a British group, we would have ignored Eurovision. But coming from Sweden, the contest was the only way of promoting ourselves in other countries. We knew that nobody would really listen to us otherwise, and so we decided to take a chance, although it could have meant that we emerged from the whole thing with a bad image".

On the subject of ABBA performing live, it had surprised many people that ABBA had not already embarked on a world tour in view of their world success. It was because of the lack of live concerts that many journalists presumed that ABBA were simply a manufactured group who would find it virtually impossible to reproduce their exceptional studio sound before a live audience. However, as Bjorn pointed out, this was not the case. "People have suggested that we don't like the idea of playing live dates, but it has been a deliberate policy. Our plan was to build up the whole ABBA image, which we have done – and make several successful records, which we have also succeeded in doing. Then we'd start doing concerts. Next year we will be doing a short British Tour, between February 10th and 14th. It will include a concert at the Royal Albert Hall in London. There will also be a European tour and then we're going to Australia, where one of our albums has sold more than 800,000 copies."

One further reason why ABBA had not commited themselves to an extensive tour was simply the time factor. "Unfortunately, it tends to be longer and longer between records" said Benny, "It becomes more difficult to put things together. For example, 'When I Kissed the Teacher' was the most difficult song to make. It was made in different ways before we found the right version. Each song on 'Arrival' required approximately one week in the studio. Altogether, we spent at least two months' effective time in the studio."
Such is the importance of studio time to ABBA, Bjorn releaved ABBA's plans to build their own recording studio, in Stockholm, "The main problem at the moment is that we can't always get into the studio when we like, because other people are using it, so having our own facilites will help considerably."

When the line of questioning turned towards ABBA's thoughts of England, Bjorn was pleased to say "I think that this was the first time we've come over to England and were met with some sort of resposne – now you seem to believe that we are not just a one-hit group, and that we are something that is serious and something that will continue."
This was something that nobody could disagree with, but why had it taken England so long to accept ABBA in the same way as countries all over the world had? Once again, Bjorn gave ABBA's thoughts on the subject, and said "Our difficultiy was to get rid of the Eurovision stamp, but I think we've successfully done that now. All round the world, they never refer to us as a Eurovision group any more, but it's still been especially hard in England because you are very much used to groups coming over from the Continent and not lasting very long. We thought that it would be extremely difficult, but sooner or later we knew that it was bound to happen. Fortunately we have been proved right."

Despite being finally accepted in England, ABBA were still faced with prejudice, espeically when it came to performing on television. "When we are over here to do Top of the Pops, we aren't allowed to use tapes, for example. The Union has deciced that British bands should work on television in the first place. For this reason, we must either record our song with the Top of the Pops orchestra, before the broadcast, or sing it live. But British bands can use tapes, since they generally make their records with English stuido musicians. When we appeared on an ITV programme in Manchester, we were on just before the British group, Queen. Queen used playback and we didn't have any time to rehears at all. The results were predictable, ours sounded awful while theirs sounded great."

It was because of these Union restrictions that ABBA would not be performing on television during this particular visit to England. Instead they concentrated on press and radio

ABBA
72

On Saturday 16th November, ABBA spent the day at IBC Radio Studios in London, where they were interviewed by Radio Hallam's Keith Skues. The interview was to be included in an ABBA Radio Special that was to be broadcasted during the forthcoming Christmas holidays by England's independent radio stations. When ABBA returned to Sweden on Monday 18th November, 'ABBAMANIA' was sweeping across England like a whirlwind. Better still, it showed no signs of slowing down. For the remainder of 1976 ABBA isolated themselves from the world so that they could concentrate on rehearsals for their forthcoming European/Australian Tour. The hype surrounding ABBA's tour was enormous, but nobody could have anticipated the phenomenal demand for tickets when they went on sale in late November.

In Sweden 18,000 tickets were sold within hours for ABBA's concert at Gothenburg's Scandanavium. In Denmark more than 2,000 people queued in the street for tickets for ABBA's concert at Copenhagen's Brondbyhallen – 10,000 tickets were sold in two hours. Such was the demand for tickets in Denmark that Knud Thorbjornson, ABBA's tour promoter, managed to persaude ABBA to play an extra concert in Copenhagen, after receiving numerous blank cheques from people desperately wanting tickets. In Australia an amazing 42,000 tickets were sold in just one day. The same story was repeated in Norway, Germany and Holland, where tickets sold at the same rate. But the most astonishing statistics came from England.

Tickets for ABBA's concert at the world famous Royal Albert Hall, in London, were only available by mail order, so people were invited to send in their ticket applications. For the 11,212 tickets available, a phenomenal 3.5 million ticket applications were received. England's N.M.E. revealed that ABBA could fill the Royal Albert Hall 624 times. In early December a malicious rumour concerning ABBA spread through Europe, causing ABBA and their fans much distress. A news report from Germany stated that all four members of ABBA had been killed when their plane crash-landed at Templehof Airport, West Berlin. As news of 'ABBA's' deaths' spread from country to country, the original report changed. When it reached Holland and England, it stated that only three members of ABBA had been killed, the survivor being Frida. However, she was so badly injured that should would never sing again.

ABBA immediately took action to ensure the rumours would stop. Polar Music in Stockholm contacted all ABBA's European record companies to dismiss the rumours, and Bjorn came 'out of hiding' to appear on German television. It did not take long for the rumours to die. As the Christmas festivities began, not even malicious rumours could prevent ABBA from celebrating their busiest and most successful year. Twelve months earlier ABBA had been the rising stars of the international music world. Today they were international superstars.

CHAPTER ELEVEN
EUROPEAN/AUSTRALIAN TOUR

The impact of ABBA's phenomenal world-wide appeal and success during 1976 was clear to see when, in the New Year 1977, ABBA were showered with numerous awards from around the world. Each award paid tribute to ABBA's musical talents and phenomenal record successes during 1976. In England, ABBA were named 'Top Group' by Record Mirror, whilst N.M.E. announced that ABBA were the biggest record sellers of 1976. In Hitmakers magazine, 'Arrival' was named as the year's best album.

Similar awards came in from around the world – 'Dancing Queen' was voted "top single" in Holland, whilst in Portugal 'Fernando' was voted 'best recording in 1976'. Portugal also paid tribute to Benny and Bjorn by naming them as 'top producers' and 'top songwriters'. ABBA were greatly honoured to receive every award, but were undoubtedly especially happy when they learned of an award that came from America during the first week of January. On 30th December 1976 the 500,000th copy of ABBA's 'Greatest Hits' album was sold in America – resulting in ABBA receiving their very first American R.I.A.A. gold disc award.

ABBA spent the majority of January 'locked away' in Stockholm, primarily preparing themselves and rehearsing for their forthcoming European/Australian Tour. They were also looking towards their next single release. 'Knowing Me Knowing You', which was scheduled for release in February. Owing to their tour itinerary, ABBA would not be available for promotion. It was therefore decided that 'Knowing You Knowing Me' would be released with an accompanying promotional video. Under the direction of Swedish film maker Lasse Hallstrom, ABBA spent two days in January filming the video.

On a personal level, it was during January and Agnetha and Bjorn decided that they would like to expand their family and try for another baby. However, since Agnetha and Bjorn's first child, Linda, had been born in 1973, their circumstances had changed drastically and they soon realised that Agnetha's pregnancy would have to be carefully planned. Not wanting Agnetha's pregnancy or the baby's arrival to disrupt activities surrounding ABBA the group, Agnetha and Bjorn decided that Christmas 1977 would be the most appropriate time to welcome an addition to their family. However, for the time being, ABBA the group took prominence once again.

After one year of precision planning and countless rehearsals, ABBA's first World Tour was finally ready to hit the road. The interest and hype surrounding the tour was enormous, as proved by the phenomenal demand for concert tickets. As fans lucky enough to have tickets for any one of ABBA's shows anxiously waited to see the world's top pop group perform live, the world's music critics were equally as anxious to see whether ABBA could reproduce their outstanding studio sound before a live audience. As for ABBA themselves, their priority was to deliver a show of the highest quality that their fans would remember and not forget.

ABBA had employed twelve of the best musicians available to support them on tour: Anders Elias (keyboards), Wojciech Ernest (keyboards, Lars Wellander (guitar), Finn Sjobert (guitar), Rutger Gunnarsson (bass), Malando Gassama (percussion), Ola Brunkert (drums), Ulf Andersson (saxophone), Lars Karlsson (saxophone), Lena Andersson (backing singer), Maritza Horn (backing singer) and Lena-Marie Gardenas-Lawton (backing singer). Agnetha and Frida had also employed the help of voice instructor Inga Sundstrom, to ensure that their voices were on top form for the tour.

Including the musicians and 'roadies', an entourage totalling 105 people accompanied ABBA, including: Thomas Johansson (Tour Organiser), Louise de Faire (P.A. to T. Johansson), Bo Norling (Tour Manager), Knud Thorbjornsen (Tour Promoter), hans Lofvenberg (P.A. to Bo Norling), Stefan Lundin (Stage Manager), Jimmy Barnett (Production Manager), Brian Croft (lights and effects), Joe Brown (Sound), Keith Bradley (Sound), David Kirkwood (Sound), Tasco (Sound), Ashley Williams (Sounds), Claes af Feijerstam (Sound Engineer), Owe Sandstrom (Costumers), Lars Wegenuis (Costumes), Edwin Shirley (Road Transport), Tore Bengtsson (Road Transport), Hans Blomgren (Air Transport), and Fellenius (Air Transport).

The eyes and ears of fans and critics alike would be firmly fixed on ABBA throughout their tour and so ABBA ensured that no stone was left unturned when it came to the arranging and execution of their first world tour.

During 1976, Knud Thorbjornsen worked closely with ABBA, choosing suitable venues in which ABBA could perform. Many concert halls and arenas were 'auditioned' throughout Europe and Australia before this final ininerary was reached.

EUROPEAN DATES

Date	Country	City	Venue
28.1.77	NORWAY	OSLO	EKEBERGSHALLEN
29.1.77	SWEDEN	GOTHENBURG	SCANDANAVIUM
30.1.77	SWEDEN	GOTHENBERG	SCANDANAVIUM
31.1.77	DENMARK	COPENHAGEN	BRONDBYHALLEN
1.2.77	DENMARK	COPENHAGEN	BRONDBYHALLEN
2.2.77	GERMANY	BERLIN	DEUTSCHLANDHALLE
3.2.77	GERMANY	KOLN	SPORTHALLE
4.2.77	HOLLAND	AMSTERDAM	JAAP EDEN HALL
5.2.77	BELGIUM	ANTWERP	ARENA HALL
6.2.77	GERMANY	ESSEN	GRUGAHALLE
7.2.77	GERMANY	HANNOVER	ELLENRIEDEHALLE
8.2.77	GERMANY	HAMBURG	C.C.H.
10.2.77	ENGLAND	BIRMINGHAM	ODEON
11.2.77	ENGLAND	MANCHESTER	FREE TRADE HALL
12.2.77	SCOTLAND	GLASGOW	APOLLO
14.2.77	ENGLAND	LONDON	ROYAL ALBERT HALL *(2 SHOWS)*

AUSTRALIAN DATES

3.3.77	-AUSTRALIA -	SYDNEY	-	SHOWGROUND ARENA
4.3.77	-AUSTRALIA -	SYDNEY	-	SHOWGROUND AREA
5.3.77	-AUSTRALIA -	MELBOURNE		
6.3.77	-AUSTRALIA -	MELBOURNE	-	*(3 SHOWS IN MELBOURNE)*
8.3.77	-AUSTRALIA -	ADELAIDE	-	
10.3.77	- AUSTRALIA -	PERTH	-	CENTRA
11.3.77	- AUSTRALIA -	PERTH	-	CENTRA (5 SHOWS IN PERTH)
12.3.77	- AUSTRALIA -	PERTH	-	CENTRA

With a total of 28 shows, this was the biggest and longest tour ABBA had undetaken to date, but had been planned so that, as Bjorn releaved, "It is both physically and mentally fine". It was inevitable that ABBA could have made the tour much, much longer, but due to their writing and recording commitments, together with Agnetha and Bjorn's personal plans to have another child, this itinerary was adequate to all concerned. Of course, the only people who would have liked the tour to be much longer were a few million ABBA fans who were not able to get tickets for any of the shows. However, ABBA realised that only a minority of fans would actually get to see them in concert, and so it was decided that segments of the tour would be filmed for an 'ABBA in Concert' Television Special.

January 28th arrived and ABBA premiered their long-awaited world tour in front of a sell-out audience at Oslo's Ekebergshallen. Included in the audience were the usual army of music journalists and press photographers that events such as these attact, together with representatives from the Norweigan Royal Family, namely Crown Price Harald and Crown Princess Sonja. As the concert hall was silenced by the sound of a helicopter landing, four spotlights beamed down on the darkened stage to reveal the four glittery figures of Agnetha, Benny, Bjorn and Frida. For the next hundred minutes the audience erupted, watching and listening in awe as ABBA delivered a show of musical and visual excellence. ABBA began by introducing themselves to music, with the song 'I Am An A', which was written specifically for the tour by Benny and Bjorn. From there onwards ABBA performed songs from their three albums, together with their string of hit records. As if that was not enough, and just as the audience thought they had heard all that they could have possibly hoped to hear, ABBA returned with a taste of things to come by introducing 'The Girl With The Golden Hair' – ABBA's first 'mini-musical'.

Narrated by an English Actor, 'The Girl With The Golden Hair' tells the story of a young girl singer who moves from her hometown to the city in order to find stardom. When she finally achieves the stardom she has longed for, she becomes miserable and lonely and soon learns that her only true friend is her music.

Dressed in identical blonde wigs and costumes, Agnetha and Frida portrayed the two separate personalities of the girl through four totally new ABBA songs:- 'Thank You For The Music', 'I Wonder (Departure)', 'Get On The Carousel' and 'I'm A Marionette'. Not only did 'The Girl With The Golden Hair' provide the audience with a glimpse of ABBA's musical progression, it provided everyone with an outstanding climax to a stunning show.
For the next eleven days ABBA took their show to Sweden, Denmark, Germany, Holland and Belgium, all countries in which they had performed live before. Each night the audiences went home captivated. Even Europe's music journalists were impressed by ABBA's performance with many reporting "Audiences sitting open-mouthed when they found that ABBA could reproduce their music, note for note, without a fault".

ABBA faced their biggest hurdle of the tour when, on February 9th, they arrived in England for their first-ever live shows before a British audience. ABBA had fought hard to establish themselves as a serious musical entity in England. Through their hit singles and albums, ABBA had finally earned the respect of the British audience, without the help of live peformances. However, now was the time for ABBA to show their British audience that they were as polished on stage as they were in the recording studio.

ABBA's first U.K. tour commenced at Birmingham's Odeon on 10th and then proceeded to Manchester's Free Trade Hall on 11th, Glasgow's Apollo in Scotland on 12th, before ending with two shows at London's world famous Royal Albert hall on 14th. ABBA cleared the hurdle without any problems, leaving their British audiences equally as surprised and stunned as their European neighbours had been. The English reviews, however, were as expected – mixed. Ray Coleman from Melody Maker reported that ABBA were "Cold and clinical disappointment", whilst Tony Parsons from N.M.E. described ABBA's performance as "Crass, glib and contrived".

In comparison, John Blake from the Manchester Evening News reported "ABBA are the greatest thing since The Beatles and with Anna and Frida looking the way they do, I for one would be happy even if they didn't sing a note". Regardless of what they thought of ABBA's actual performance, several critics reported on what they thought ABBA's qualities were.

"Their arrangments are their real secret, no-one in the field can match their oustandingly imaginative deployment of pianos, synthesizers and tuned percussion" wrote Richard Williams for The Times, whilst Bart Mills, writing for The Daily Mail, said "Their singles have storylines and points of view which are as true an expression of today's well-fed Europe as Chuck Berry's songs were of 1950's America."

Despite what any one individual had to say about ABBA's live performance, one sure fact was that, for the past 16 days, ABBA had entertained thousands of their fans throughout Europe, entertaining them in a way that had left them surprised, stunned and screaming for more. In that respect, ABBA had achieved what they had set out to do – nothing more, nothing less.

There was now a two week interval before the tour concluded with eleven shows in Australia. During this time ABBA returned to Stockholm to rest, reflect upon their European shows and to discuss future plans. One main topic of conversation centered around the idea of documenting the forthcoming Australian tour, in Panavision, which would then be made into a full length feature film. If everything went according to plan, ABBA would not tour at all during 1978 as Agnetha and Bjorn's baby would naturally demand much attention. It was therefore decided that an ABBA feature film would adequately compensate fans the world over the for the lack of live performances by ABBA during 1978. With the prospect of a Panavision feature film on the horizon, original plans for an 'ABBA in Concert' Television Special were axed, as Lasse hallstrom was recruited to direct this new project. It was also during this time that ABBA's new single 'Knowing Me Knowing You' was beginning to make its impact on the world charts. Promoted primarily by the accompanying video, 'Knowing Me Knowing You' was widely regarded as the strongest ABBA single to date by fans and critics alike. Within a few weeks, the song had placed ABBA back at the top of the charts around the world, reaching number one in England (where Arrival had now sold 750,000 copies), France, Germany, Austria, Finland, Switzerland, Denmark, Belgium, Luxembourg, New Zealand and The West Indies, number two in Holland, number three is Israel and number four in Australia.

The B-side of 'Knowing You Knowing Me' brought to light a new, familiar-sounding ABBA song titled 'Happy Hawaii'. Featuring Agnetha and Frida on lead vocals 'Happy Hawaii' is the early version of the Arrival album track 'Why Did It Have To Be Me', which featured Bjorn on lead vocals. Although the music is very similar on both songs, the lyrics are totally different. "Happy Hawaii is a jest on our part", revealed ABBA, "We think it's fun to show our public how we conceived the song from the beginning. And besides, many people who had heard 'Happy Hawaii' on the demo tape have wondered what happened to it."

ABBA were also making a big impact on the American charts, where their current single was 'Dancing Queen'. Early progress reports from ABBA's American Record Label, Atlantic, were very positive, indicating that 'Dancing Queen' looked like becoming a hit single all over again.

The beginning of March saw ABBA and their entourage travel to Australia for the final leg of the tour. Arriving at Sydney Airport on Thursday March 3rd, ABBA were greeted with a blaze of publicity. As press photographers fought to capture an exclusive picture of ABBA's long awaited return to Australia, thoussands of screaming fans waited hysterically outside the airport to provide ABBA with their own special welcome. For the next ten days ABBA would perform eleven shows to an estimated 150,000 people in Sydney, Melbourne, Adelaide and Perth.

Upon their arrival in Sydney, ABBA's first engagement was at their hotel, where they gave a press conference. The main line of questioning centred around ABBA's thoughts of touring and Agnetha, Benny, Bjorn and Frida all had their own views to share. Agnetha and Frida expressed their dislike of travelling.

"I think the travelling is very, very hard. One day when I woke up on the Europe tour, I started to think – where am I? In which city? And it's terrible", said Agnetha, whilst Frida announced "It's boring to travel but it's fantastic to be on stage – I really love that"
On the subject of being nervous before a performance, Benny revealed that "Every show is a bit nervous. You think you have a good performance because you had a good audience the day before – but going from Amsterdam to London or from London to Sydney, it's such a difference". He ended by saying "I'd hate the sound of 30,000 booing".

Last on the subject of touring, Bjorn said "It's a bit of an unsocial life on tour, you just eat, sleep, go on stage and nothing more. It kills creativity in a way that I don't like."
The press conference also provided some humorous moments. First came the question "Do you worry that you make money faster than you can spend it?", to which Benny replied "It's a lot of money coming in but there's a lot of tax to pay if you're a Swedish citizen. But it's still a mater of hard work and the money isn't that important really. It's more a matter of pleasing yourselves in what you are doing – we can't do anything else in the future apart from keeping ourselves happy in our work.

The second question, directed at Agnetha, referred to an article that a Swedish journalist had recently written in which he declared that Agnetha had "the sexiest bottom in showbusiness". When asked "Is it true?", an amused Agnetha replied, "How can I answer that? I don't know – I haven't seen it".

After the press conference ABBA immediately began preparing themselves for their debut live performance before an Australian audience. As 20,000 hysterical fans assembled inside Sydney's open air Showground Arena, weather conditions could not have been much worse. Strong winds blew and torrential rain poured from the sky, leaving the audience soaked to the skin and the stage covered with water. With weather conditions outside their control, ABBA could do nothing except adopt the well-known phrase "the show must go on" and perform. ABBA took to the stage and Bjorn greeted the Sydney audience, saying "You make us forget the rain – I just hope that we can make you forget it too". The audience showed their approval – nothing was going to stop them from enjoying the following ninety minutes of music.

However, the potential danger ABBA faced by performing on a water covered stage soon became evident when, during a dance routine, Frida slipped in a puddle which caused her to fall over rather awkwardly on her hands and knees. Fortunately she was only bruised and was able to continue with the performance.

Despite everything, ABBA could not have wished for a better reception from an audience, their first live show in Australia was a resounding success. The following day, reviews, photographs and stories of ABBA were the leading headlines in the Australian newspapers and magazines. However, the most astounding piece of journalism came from an 'underground' magazine based in Sydney. The magazine stated that the four people in Australia at the moment, claiming to be ABBA, were in fact actors, being paid to imitate the real ABBA.

Immediately after their second and final show in Sydney's Showground Arena on Friday evening, ABBA and their entourage travelled to Melbourne, where a weekend filled with a further three shows lay ahead of them (one on Saturday and two on Sunday), In Melbourne the Authorities were so pleased to welcome the world's top pop group to their city that a Civic Reception had been arranged for ABBA. Held on Saturday, ABBA were more than happy to attend the reception as 'guests of honour'.

Monday was a rest day in the sense that ABBA were not performing that day. Instead they travelled to Adelaide where, on Tuesday, they would perform two shows instead of the scheduled one.

"The sexiest bottom in showbusiness"

ABBA's show in Adelaide was to be the biggest of the tour in terms of audience capacity: some 40,000 tickets had been sold. However, it was decided that ABBA would perform an extra show in Adelaide so that the audience capacity could be reduced to 20,000 people per show. By doing this, any danger of injury through overcrowding would be eliminated. In 1973 a young girl was crushed to death at a similar sized concert in London. ABBA and Stig wanted to ensure that no similar danger would exist at one of their shows. After spending Wednesday resting and travelling, ABBA's final three days in Australia were spent in Perth. Here ABBA performed the final five shows of their first world tour. During their first show at Perth's 'Centra' on Thursday 10th, ABBA were forced to abandon the stage after a bomb scare threat was received. Eventually the threat was found to be a hoax and ABBA resumed their performance, much to the delight of the rather anxious audience.

The final show in Perth on Saturday 12th marked the end of ABBA's first world tour. From the first show in Oslo on January 28th to the last, here in Perth, ABBA had travelled to eight countries and performed to an estimated 300,000 people. Now ABBA could happily relex and welcome a degree of normality back to their lives, knowing that their first world tour had been a phenomenal success.

However, if a rather ambitious music promoter from Singapore had had his way, ABBA would have had one more curtain call to make. Whilst in Perth ABBA received a telegram, it read, "Understand you conclude your Australian tour in Perth. Interested in arranging an ABBA concert in Singapore. You can depart Perth so you arrive Singapore 1600hrs, so concert can take place 1930 hours same evening. Departure Singapore thus possible Tuesday morning. Please confirm your interest."

On Sunday 13th ABBA travelled back home to Sweden, but not before making their last public appearance in Australia at Perth's Moonba Festival. Thousands of people turned out to wave farewell to ABBA and to catch a last glimpse of their favourite band. As ABBA boarded their aeroplane, once again they were leaving the country where ABBAMANIA ruled above anything else.

CHAPTER TWELVE
THE MAKING OF THE MOVIE

The person responsible for ABBA's transformation to the silver screen was Lasse Hallstrom. Lasse had been making films since he was eleven years old and today was one of Sweden's top film directors. Working primarily for Swedish Television, Lasse was also the person responsible for all of ABBA's promotional videos, his most recent work being the acclaimed video for 'Knowing Me Knowing You'. Now Lasse was undertaking his most ambitious project to date, ABBA's first feature film to be called simply 'ABBA The Movie'. The object of the movie was to document, in Panavision, ABBA's tour of Australia. Combining on-stage action with off-stage action. The Movie would provide ABBA fans the world over with the opportunity of seeing ABBA in concert during 1978 via the silver screen. Taking the place of another world tour, the movie would allow ABBA to stay at home in Stockholm for the majority of 1978 so that they could concentrate on family and creative commitments.

From the moment ABBA arrived in Australia, Lasse, together with a film crew totalling approximately one hundred people, were there with ABBA, capturing the unfolding events on film. A last-minute decision by Lasse to include a simple storyline within the movie resulted in three Australian actors being employed to portray the characters in the script written by Lasse. The story centered around a radio station disc jockey called Ashley, played by Robert Hughes. Ashley is assigned by his radio station manager (Bruce Barry) to get an exclusive, in-depth interview with ABBA whilst they are in Australia. With a deadline of one week, Ashley follows ABBA across Australia in search of an interview. Every time Ashley gets within talking distance of ABBA he is quickly stopped from getting any closer by their bodyguard (Tom Oliver). With the deadline quickly running out, Ashley becomes determined to achieve his goal, whatever it takes. Will Ashley be granted an exclusive, in-depth interview? Or will all his efforts result in failure? All will be revealed in The Movie. Whatever the outcome, the exploits of Ashley provide 'The Movie' with an amusing sideline.

Throughout the filming of 'The Movie', Lasse and his crew's skill and patience were put to the test. "We have two film crews and two extra photographers. An unbelievable stack of equipment had to be packed, moved, un-packed and re-packed at every concert location on ABBA's tour. There were times when ABBA's own personal guards – we filmers called them 'gorillas', lost track of who was who. I found myself forcibly restrained from getting close on several occasions. I got a little tired of having to explain that I was there at ABBA's own request", revealed Lasse.

Another person to fall victim to the ABBA 'gorillas' was actor Robert Hughes, as he explains: "On one occasion I had to make a rush for ABBA as they came out of their tour caravan – and would you believe it, nobody had told the bodyguards. I got clobbered right away and a glorious fight started. I was so glad when someone eventually convinced those guys that I was the actor."

This was one incident that could possibly have been avoided if Robert's identity was known to ABBA and their bodyguards. However, wanting 'The Movie' to be as 'natural' as possible, Lasse had purposely kept Robert's identity a secret. Although ABBA and their entourage were aware of the storyline, it took them a while to realise that Robert was in fact Ashley. "We wondered who this odd, pushy journalist was. He kept asking strange questions all the time and always wanted us to go somewhere where it was a little quieter. To tell you the truth, we got kind of fed up with him. We cottoned-on in the end though, and it makes us all laugh now to think how we treated poor Robert", revealed Frida. Despite everything, when ABBA left Australia on March 13th, Lasse had twenty hours of footage 'in the can'. Amid great secrecy, the last scenes for 'The Movie' were filmed in Sweden during June. The final outdoor sequences were filmed on the idyllic island of Djurgarden in central Stockholm whilst indoor sequences were filmed in a studio. Roberth Hughes and Tom Oliver were imported from Australia, and for one particular sequence, ABBA invited some of Stockholm's senior citizens, students and unemployed to act as 'film extras'. Once again, Lasse's skill and patience was put to the test during filming in Sweden. "There was one particularly difficult scene which has ABBA in a lift, singing 'Eagle'. We had to invent a completely new apparatus to shoot that one", said Lasse. "Then there was the bit where ABBA, starting from the distant part of the studio, came into the foreground through a very complicated system of mirrors. That one almost had me climbing the walls."

However, it was during the filming of these sequences for 'Eagle' that Lasse was proud to be the first person ever to use a newly invented device called the 'flutter box'. The "flutter box" created spectacular effects involving fluttering coloured lights, and had been invented specifically for the new Superman movie. Lasse claimed it first, and 'ABBA The Movie' is the very first production in the world to use this new device. In July, Lasse, together with Malou Hallstrom and Ulf Neidemar, began editing 'The Movie'. With ABBA's first feature film finally nearing completion, Lasse was asked, "How does it feel?" to which he simply replied "Kind of pleasant".

CHAPTER THIRTEEN
AWAY FROM IT ALL

With their first world tour successfully completed, ABBA now needed to isolate themselves from the world so that they could devote themselves to recording their next album. Firstly, Benny and Bjorn needed peace and quiet in order to write new material for ABBA, so Stig issued the following statement to the world's press: "ABBA are not available for anything from 1st April until October."

Also on a personal level, Agnetha was now pregnant and needed to take things easy in order to ensure her pregnancy would be stress-free and as comfortable as possible. Above all else, ABBA needed a well-earned rest from their hectic workload so that they could all spend some precious time with their family, friends and children. To quote Bjorn, "Understand us – we are not toys, we have a desperate need to have peace and quiet to work. People scratch and pull us from all sides, therefore we have to say no to interivews, etc. We do not want to be destroyed by Showbusiness – we want a private life to spend time with the kids, so sometimes you have to be tough and say no."

Despite Agnetha, Benny, Bjorn and Frida's temporary withdrawal from public engagements, the worldwide progression of ABBA continued. At the beginning of April ABBA learned that a group dream had finally become a reality. ABBA had finally achieved their very first number one single in America with 'Dancing Queen'. On April 4th, 'Dancing Queen' had sold its millionth American copy, resulting in ABBA's being awarded their first American gold disc for a single. Within a few weeks they received another gold disc from America – this time it was for one million sales of their 'Arrival' album.

It was also during April that construction work began on an old cinema in central Stockholm. Recently bought by ABBA, the cinema was being transformed into ABBA's very own recording studio. American recording studio expert Tom Hidley was employed to take charge of the design and construction of the studio which, when completed, would be the world's most modern and techncially advanced recording studio.

"We are not involved too much with the business side of things"

During the summer months, ABBA recorded their new album at Marcus and Metronome Studios in Stockholm. Agnetha, who was now well into her pregnancy, continued to rest as much as possible and so only worked in the mornings. This meant Frida recorded some vocals that would normally have been recorded by Agnetha.

With ABBA continuing to isolate themselves from the world, the world's press were beginning to search frantically for ABBA-related stores to report upon. Many newspapers and magazines began reporting about the international business and financial deals that Polar Music, ABBA's own record company, were now negotiating.

The enormous financial income that ABBA's phenomenal record sales were generating resulted in Polar Music being declared the most profitable corporation in Sweden. Primarily instigated by Stig and various business associates, the business and financial dealing surrounding ABBA make fascinating reading. However, it became very important to Agnetha, Benny, Bjorn and Frida that ABBA the group should be kept totally separate from any business and financial deals made with ABBA money. "We are not involved too much with the business side of things" said Bjorn, "Music takes up all of our time. Our work is to write, record and perform songs. That's what we like doing and that is the main thing, so we try to keep away from the business side. But when there's a big decison to be made, we all sit down and discuss it with the other people because we obviously have to say what we think."

In August, Stig issued another statement to the world's press, saying that ABBA had now sold 50 million records worldwide, 30 albums and 20 million singles. This statement led to more press coverage for ABBA with many newspapers reporting that ABBA were now "bigger than The Beatles". On a pesonal level, perhaps the most interesting and important press reports concerned Frida.

In their search for ABBA-related stories, many newspapers and magazines began printing details of Frida's childhood. The story of how Frida's mother, Synni, had died at the age of twenty-one after being deserted by Frida's father, a German soldier by the name of Alfred Haase, make for compulsive reading. Frida believed that her father, Alfred, had been killed at the end of the war when his ship back to Germany had been sunk. When the story appeared in the German magazine Bravo, it was read by ABBA fan Andrea Buchinger. Andrea immediately recognised the name Alfred Haase as she had an uncle of the same name. She was also aware that her uncle had served in Norway as a soldier during the war. Andrea immediately telephoned her cousin Peter and told him of the coincidence. Peter then proceeded to ask his father if he had known a young girl called Synni Lyngstad whilst he was in Norway during the war. It soon became evident that this Alfred Haase, now living in Karlsruhe, Germany with his family, must be Frida's father.

Alfred had in fact returned safely to Germany after the war and upon his return had begun writing to Synni. However, due to post-war confusion, none of his letters were delivered. After not receiving any reply from Synni, Alfred presumed that she was no longer interested in him. Not only was Alfred unaware that Synni was expecting their child, he did not know that Synni had died and that their daughter was being raised in Sweden by Synni's mother. In Stockholm, Frida was unaware of the developments taking place in Karlsruhe, Germany, tunil she received a telephone call at Polar Music from Alfred. At first the situation was very tense, as they did not share a common language. But when an employee at Polar Music who spoke German acted as translator, indisputable facts were checked which left Frida and Alfred in no doubt they were father and daughter.

Within days, Frida and Alfred had met for the first time. "When I realised that my father was alive after all, I cried and cried for hours. Then I couldn't sleep for days until I had seen him for myself. We have so many family similarities, the same noses, same hands. When I walked barefoot through my house, he took off his socks and shoes and we laughed. We even have the same sort of feet" recalled Frida.

CHAPTER FOURTEEN
THE SILENCE IS BROKEN

On October 14th, ABBA broke their six-month silence and released a new single titled 'The Name of the Game'. Taken from the forthcoming album, it was an immediate hit, reaching number one in England, Germany, Sweden, Switzerland, Austria, Finland and Luxembourg, and number two in Australia, New Zealand, Holland and The West Indies.

Being longer than any of ABBA's previous single releases, 'The Name OF The Game' was sure proof of ABBA's musical progression and was well received by critics. England's Sounds magazine wrote "A satisfying emotive chord sequence and the usual superb vocal harmonies and production", whilst Melody Maker declared, "Not a classic but it will more than do."

The B-side was also a track from the forthcoming album titled 'I Wonder (Departure)'. This particular version had been recorded live when ABBA performed at the Showground Arena, Sydney, during their recent Australian Tour.

Even with the release of a new single ABBA remained in Stockholm, as 'The Name Of The Game' was primarily promoted by an accompanying video directed, as always, by Lasse Hallstrom. By the end of October ABBA's new album, titled simply 'ABBA The Album', together with 'ABBA The Movie', were finally completed. As both were being pressed, time proved to be ABBA's biggest enemy. Originally ABBA had intended to release 'The Album' and 'The Movie' simultaneously during December. But advance-orders for The Album were so phenomenal that it was going to be impossible to press enough copies before the scheduled release date. The same problem was encountered with 'The Movie'. "We're aiming to release 'The Movie' around Christmas time but much will depend on how many copies can be made before December" said Stig.

As December arrived, Agnetha entered the final stages of her pregnancy and on the 4th she gave birth to a healthy baby boy at Stockholm hospital. Four days later Agnetha and Bjorn proudly introduced their son, Peter Christian, to an army of press photographers. Obviously unimpressed with all the attention, Peter Christian calmly slept throughout the proceedings. The remaining weeks of December saw 'ABBA The Album' being released in Sweden, where advance orders totalled an amazing 600,000 copies. On December 17th, 'ABBA The Movie' received its world premiere at the Amsterdam City Theatre, Holland, before being released in Australia and Sweden. The rest of the world would have to wait until 1978 before sampling the latest ABBA products.

CHAPTER FIFTEEN
MOVING ON

As 1978 arrived, it came as much relief to Agnetha, Benny, Bjorn and Frida that this year ABBA would not be undertaking any concert tours or live performances whatsoever. Instead, ABBA would be promoted and seen around the world via their new album, 'The Movie' and various scheduled televsion appearances. With this major reduction in ABBA's travel commitments, Agnetha, Benny, Bjorn and Frida were all looking forward to a less hectic and stressful year. "We really need a rest this year. There is a limit to what we can take in the way of touring, and just to grab ourselves some relaxation and some family life will be pure heaven" said Agnetha.

On January 13th, 'ABBA The Album' was unveiled to the world. Recorded at Marcus and Metronome Studios, Stockholm, 'The Album' contained nine new songs – 'Eagle', 'Take A Chance On Me', 'One Man One Woman', 'The Name Of The Game', 'Move On', 'Hole In Your Soul', plus three songs from ABBA's mini-musical, 'The Girl With The Golden Hair', i.e. 'Thank You For The Music', 'I Wonder (Departure)' and 'I'm A Marionette'. Worldwide advance orders for 'The Album' were phenomenal, especially in England where it entered the charts at number one after sales had exceeded one million pounds prior to its release.

Once again, the majority of critics were very negative with their views. Whilst most were in agreement that 'Eagle', 'Take A Chance On Me', 'One Man One Woman' and 'The Name Of The Game' revealed ABBA at their best, many felt that the remaining songs were less than satisfactory. Melody Maker ended its review by saying, "Probably ABBA's weakest album since they first hit the big time", whilst N.M.E. agreed by saying "Could turn out to be ABBA's least satisfactory album". Being rather more postive, America's Rolling Stone magazine said "Side two is a real attempt to do something different and, if not everything works, the effort is still laudable."

Regardless of what any one critic had to say, 'The Album' was a resounding success around the world and showed without any doubt that ABBA were the most progressive creators of pop music in the world today. To coincide with the release of The Album on January 27th, ABBA released their new single, 'Take A Chance On Me'/'I'm A Marionette', together with the usual accompanying promotional video. Despite being included on 'The Album', 'Take A Chance On Me' was an immediate worldwide hit. In England it became ABBA's seventh single to top the charts, and also reached the number one position in France, Germany, Austria, Sweden, Denmark, Switzerland and Luxembourg.

With the release of their latest album, Benny and Bjorn wasted no time in writing for ABBA's next album. As Benny and Bjorn began searching for inspiration, Agnetha occupied herself with her children whilst Frida generally took things easy for a while. However, during February ABBA ventured outside of Sweden for a series of promotional visits to coincide with various European premieres of ABBA The Movie. Firstly ABBA attended a special preview of 'The Movie' at Cannes in France, where they also attended the MIDEM music business gathering. Then on February 16th, ABBA arrived in England for four days' promotion to coincide with the international release of 'The Movie'.

The evening of the 16th saw ABBA travel to the Warner Cinema in London's West End where 'The Movie' was receiving its international premiere. As ABBA arrived, thousands of fans crowded the streets to greet them. Inside the cinema the scene was equally chaotic. Journalists, photographers, celebrities, fellow artists and musicians, together with lucky fans, had all turned out to watch ABBA's latest offering with the stars themselves. After sitting through two hours of ABBA in glorious Panavision, the invited people made their way to the Café Royal in Regent Street, where a celebratory reception was being held. Here ABBA spoke to journalists and mixed with fellow guests, but not before being presented with an array of platinum, gold and silver disc awards for their latest record successes in England.

Naturally many journalists asked questions with regard to 'The Movie'. "We really do need a rest this year and The Movie will provide it for us. We hope that The Movie will keep us in the spotlight, so to speak, while we work on other longer-term plans" commented Frida.

ABBA were also asked, in turn, to give their own personal views of 'The Movie'. "I really liked the idea from the beginning", said Agnetha, "And now I've seen the film for the first time, I can see that I was right. I'm very pleased with the result. I really do appreciate the scenes with the children. Having children of your own makes such scenes really funny". Firda also though that 'The Movie' was a good idea right from the start. However, Benny and Bjorn were less optimistic. "We were very suspiscious right from the beginning, especially me" said Benny, "I had my reasons because of the flop we had with The Hep Stars. That was my first experience with film and it didn't leave much desire to get invovled with it again. For a long time my attitude towards 'The Movie' was negative, so much so that I didn't want to allow Lasse to shoot on stage during the concerts – I thought the film crew would disrupt us and the audience. After seeing just how well these sequences were turning out, I understood that 'The Movie' was very different from The Hep Stars' 'Nairobi' catastrophe and changed my mind." Bjorn began by saying "Seeing 'The Movie' came as a bit of a shock. It's hard to recognise yourself up there on a giant screen in Panavision. But then we've had many moments when it has been hard to accept the things that have been happening to us". However, he ended by saying "Quite honestly, I don't think that films with pop stars work very well. Of course The Beatles are an exception and 'Tommy' was a big hit, but there have been lots of other films that have sunk without a trace."

"So many stars who allow themselves to become too much of a public property find themselves burned out in a glare of publicity."

Another main question asked of ABBA was "How do you rate your chances of survival?", to which Bjorn replied "We seen no reason to be alarmed about our future. For one thing we are two pairs rather than four individuals and we were all friends before we ever thought of forming a group. We have managed to keep our private lives reasonably private too, which I think adds to our chances. So many stars who allow themselves to become too much of a public property find themselves burned out in a glare of publicity."

When asked the same question, Benny revealed "Everything has to end sometime. We have doubts each time we release a record. We think 'this could be the last big one'. If we produced something that we really believed in and it made no impact on the charts, we'd be scared." The final questions directed to ABBA concerned their individual ambitions outside ABBA. Frida revealed "I have an ambition to sing opera and I'm currently taking singing lessons", whilst Agnetha confessed her desire to be an actress "I would consider the offer of making a film very seriously, although in fact I have recently turned down one producer. We wanted me for the kind of rude film for which Sweden has become rather notorious." Benny and Bjorn's ambition was a combined one: "What we would like to do is write a musical – this had been our dream for many years" they said.

The following day the critics made their views of 'The Movie' known via their various newspapers and magazines. Derek Jewell from The Times wrote "This movie will stun you. ABBA themselves – by heaven, such impact! Were ever a group more wholesomely handsome? The men, very hairy and Vikingesque, master musicians; the girls, beautiful and talented, and with endowments so additional as to mock any principles of fair play for us mere mortals. See it this month and marvel."

In another review headed "Appetising ABBA Delight" Kenneth Baily wrote "Artful filming radiates the clean freshness and superb showmanship of ABBA and one forgets that this is virtually a 90-minute commercial. No less than 25 numbers play out a rich feast of the ABBA sound. Performed during a tour of Australia, repetition of concert hall ovations and rapid shots of performance don't become tiring because the film scans intimately the artistry of the group as individuals. Agnetha's sexy looks are amusingly engaging, never salacious. Frida is exciting, emotionally energetic in her songs. Benny is all reassuring good humour and Bjorn shows cool enterprise. Together the overwhelming likeableness of ABBA is astutely rammed home."

"What we would like to do is write a musical –this had been our dream for many years"

Radio and Record News paid tribute to director Lasse Hallstrom in their review. Describing the photography as 'superb', it also commented that "The dream sequence featuring Ashley having a picnic with ABBA was brilliantly executed in every aspect of cinematography." There were, however, the usual negative reviews. N.M.E. said "This full-blow epic is shockingly bad, providing the ABBA fan with an embarassingly feeble plot to offset the preponderance of ABBA music", whilst Sounds remarked "Everything is fine about ABBA, except the film they have made – it's awful."

It is interesting the note that five songs featured in 'The Movie' have not been recorded by ABBA. 'Johan Pa Snippen', 'Polken Gar' and 'Stoned' are all traditional Swedish folk songs. The remaining two, 'Please Change Your Mind' and 'Get On The Carousel' are Andersson/Ulvaeus compositions. However, 'Please Change Your Mind' is an instrumental and was performed in 'The Movie' by Nashville Train. 'Get On Your Carousel' is the fourth song of ABBA's mini' musical, 'The Girl With The Golden Hair', but since Benny and Bjorn 'stole' parts of it for other songs, it remains unrecorded by ABBA.

For the remaining three days of their visit to London, ABBA concentrated on solid promotion. As well as making several appearances on television, ABBA talked to the press and were also interviewed for national Radio One by Dave Lee Travis.

One highlight of ABBA's visit came when Princess Margaret presented them with the Carl Alan Award for 'Top Group' at London's Lyceum Ballroom. When asked by a journalist the customary question on such occasions, "What did Her Royal Highness say to you?', Bjorn replied "she was very nice, but she didn't say whether or not she was an ABBA fan". Before returning to Sweden, ABBA stopped over in Germany, where they attended the German premiere of 'The Movie'.

Back home in Sweden, Benny and Bjorn immediately began writing new material whilst Agnetha and Frida began designing new outfits for ABBA, together with their fashion designer Christer Lindarw. "We're busy choosing fabrics and designs for new outfits which we will wear for TV or stage appearances when the time comes to promote the new album. Things have to be done a long way in advance if everything is to be ready on time" revealed Frida, and continued by saying "If Benny and Bjorn had anything to do with the stage clothes, we'd still be wearing the same stuff we had back in '74, because like most men, they hate shopping and are happy to wear the first thing that comes to hand." During March ABBA turned their attentions to the American market.

On 10th March, 'ABBA The Album' was certified Gold in America, after selling 500,000 copies. This came as good news, especially as Stig was currently arranging a huge promotional campaign for ABBA throughout America. It was decided that May would be declared 'ABBA Month' in America and to ensure ABBA would receive maximum exposure, Stig had employed the help of American's leading 'starmakers', the Scotti Brothers. "By and large, the US still remains for us to conquer. We've racked up good sales over the last few years, our albums get into the top forty, and some of our singles have done even better than that, like 'Dancing Queen', which was number one, but we still haven't broken down the heaviest doors, so to speak. To be frank, we're not the household name in America that we'd like to be" said Stig. It was also during March that ABBA's 'official' fan magazine in England ran a series of 'off the cuff' interviews with Agnetha, Benny, Bjorn and Frida. For the first time, ABBA gave their fans an interesting insight to their personal lives, likes and dislikes, covering a whole array of subjects:

CLOTHES
AGNETHA – "I like clothes I can feel comforable in, jeans and pullovers. Colours? Blue, white, red and black, but mostly blue and white. I also prefer boots to shoes. Make up? At home I scarcely ever wear any. I think it's better for the skin to do without and I don't like painting myself up too much but for TV, of course, one has to do so to a certain extent."

FRIDA – "I am very aware of fashion and I keep in touch with new trends through magazines, talking to designers and of course through looking around shops. I like to think of myself as fashion-conscious without being a slave to fashion. I go mostly for the more elegant style though there is a little bit of the 'hippy' in me that makes me want to mix things up so that they don't look too formal. As far as colours are concerned, I go for both strong and soft colours, my choice largely depending on my mood at the time."

BENNY – "I'm not all that interested in clothes though I'm glad we don't have to wear those flashy stage costumes any more. Nobody ever bothers to ask me my opinion when it comes to choosing stage outfits because they know I'm not much use at that sort of thing. I just like to be comfortable and look all right."

TELEVISION

BJORN – "Agnetha says I'm a TV addict but it isn't really true. I watch the news and the odd series. At the moment, I'm watching 'All you Need Is Love', the documentary series on the history of popular music. I'm really enjoying it."

AGNETHA – "In Sweden it isn't much good, so I hardly watch anything. The news maybe or a good film if there's one on. I watch more TV when I'm in England."

BENNY – "I don't watch it much because Swedish TV isn't very good. I see the news every day and any good old movies they put on, but that's about it."

FILMS/CINEMA

AGNETHA – "I like to go to the movies and we sometimes go and see a Swedish film when we can get a babysitter. I like all kinds of films, but I think Polanski is probably my favourite director. Favourite actors? There are so many, Jack Nicholson, Liv Ullman, Burton and Taylor, and lots more."

FRIDA – "I enjoy going to the cinema. I like most kinds of films, depending on my mood. I have a special preference for thrillers. Favourite actors? Jack Nicholson among the men and women, there are so many I would not want to name an outright favourite."

BENNY – "I loved 'Close Encounters', which is the only film I've seen recently. At the moment I've got a list of films I'm dying to see – 'Julia', 'Annie Hall', 'The Goodbye Girl' and 'Saturday Night Fever'. The trouble is all good films tend to come at once. Favourite actors? I've got lots: Richard Burton, Jack Nicholson, Vanessa Redgrave, Julie Christie, Ellen Burstein . . ."

BJORN – "I'm dying to see 'Close Encounters'. I'm a science fiction freak especially, but I like most films, except those French and Italian-style love stories where everyone talks all through the film and nothing every happens."

TRAVEL/HOLIDAYS

AGNETHA – "I don't like flying. I always get frightened and I wouldn't fly at all if I didn't have to. Places to go for a holiday? I'd like to go to Hawaii, Honolulu and Texas. I'd really like to go to Texas! I'd like to go and see something that I have not seen before."

FRIDA – "I like to travel, even by air, which poor Agnetha hates, though she fights valiantly against her nervousness. As far as places to travel to are concerned, I would love to return to the West Indies. There is one particular island I long to visit, which friends have told me about. So far it is completely unexploited and I want to get there before it starts to get ruined."

BJORN – "I like to be near water, the sea, rivers. I also love mountains and I'm very fond of the English countryside."

COLLECTING

BENNY – "I'm not a great collector of anything. I'm fond of modern art and have bought one or two nice prints, but not enough to call myself an art collector by any means."

FRIDA – "I think I am the one member of ABBA who does collect something. I go for salt and pepper pots and over the past three or four years I have amassed quite a collection of them, of all kinds and from many different parts of the world. I also collect chess pieces, for which there are some fantastic and beautiful designs these days.

FOOD AND DRINK

AGNETHA – "I love food: French food, Chinese food, Japanese food and spring food. My only problem is that I have to be very careful not to eat too much. I enjoy cooking myself, when I get the time, and Bjorn can cook well, too. Drink? I drink whisky, champagne and I'm very fond of good red wine and milk."

BENNY – "I like all good, well-cooked food. The only things I don't eat are spinach and offal. I do a little cooking myself, but not a great deal."

FRIDA – "I'm really a very sociable kind of person, so I love to go out to nice restaurants. I like most kinds of foods, but Italian and French cooking especially, as well as lots of Swedish cuisine. To drink I almost invariably have either white wine or champagne."

MUSIC

FRIDA – "A lot of things depend on my mood and the same goes for music. I like most kinds of music when I am in the mood for them, but at the moment I seem to be listening mostly to opera on the classical side and soul on the modern."

BENNY – "Music is a very large part of my life. I listen to records a great deal and to every kind of music except modern jazz. I also play the piano a lot, to amuse myself. I have a lot of favourite classical composers, particularly Tchaikovsky, Mozart, Bach and Beethoven. Among modern musicans I like Fleetwood Mac, the more recent stuff the Bee Gees have been doing, Rod Stewart and Stevie Wonder. I also listen to a lot of records that are in the charts to keep in touch with what is going on."

BJORN – "I have a wonderful collection at home called 'The Best of Karajan' who, of course, is one of the world's greatest conductors. I like many different classical composers – Bach, Mozart, Brahms, Beethoven – and this collection has something by all of them and the recordings are excellent. At the moment I'm listening to 'Saturday Night Fever' a lot. I also like Rod Stewart very much and The Eagles. I like to hear as much new music as possible. We get all the new American and British chart entries sent to us each week so that we can keep up with what's happening. Punk Rock? I thought it was just about finished. It is, isn't it? Some of the hit singles, like The Sex Pistols' 'God Save the Queen', did have a certain energy, but it's not really my kind of music. I should imagine that it is very hard for groups to find new hit songs within that format. Frida and Agnetha met Johnny Rotten at Stockholm Airport and he came over and said he liked ABBA."

MARRIAGE/DIVORCE
AGNETHA – "The divorce rate is very high in Sweden and it's very bad if children are involved. I don't think that marriage is that important any more. Many of my friends are just happy living together, but I do feel that some people don't try hard enough to make their marriages work."

SPORT
BJORN – "My favourite sport is cross-country skiing, although I can only do that for about three months of the year. The rest of the time I just like doing some jogging to keep fit."

FRIDA – "I am not a frightfully sporty person although I enjoy swimming. As a spectator, I am very keen on tennis. I love the outdoors and most of all, I love being on the sea."

BENNY – "I'm a sports freak. I follow all sports, especially ice-hockey and football. Do I play sports? Yes, a little tennis, but mostly I like to watch the experts playing sports."

WOMEN'S RIGHTS
AGNETHA – "I could say plenty in Swedish, but I'm note sure my English is up to it. It's easy for women's rights to go too far. People should be trying to help each other to be good humans, instead of squabbling over whose role is what, and where the demarcation lines should be drawn."

TOURING
AGNETHA – "Maybe I shouldn't really say so, but I hate it. All the travelling, living out of a suitcase and so on. I don't even enjoy the concerts themselves, because there are always too many things to worry about that could go wrong. There is an enormous pressure and frankly I sometimes find it very hard to take."

During the first week of April, ABBA travelled to Paris for a short promotional visit, prior to the French premiere of The Movie. Although they did not attend the premiere itself, ABBA made various television appearances combined with radio and press interviews. Bjorn was delighted that he would not have to attend another premiere presentation of 'The Movie'. He said "I'm very glad that we didn't have to go to the premiere itself, because I've seen the film about five times now and it's quite enough for me. I keep thinking of the things I would like to have done rather differently and so I think it's best now to stay away from it and not let it bother me."

The final week of April saw ABBA travelling once again. This time they were heading for Los Angeles for the launch of America's 'ABBA month'. For the next ten days, ABBA would be concentrating one hundred percent on promoting themselves throughout America. Since it was decided to declare May 'ABBA month' in America, Stig, the Scotti Brothers and ABBA's American record company, Atlantic, had devised a magnificent and spectacular promotional campaign which would ensure that ABBA received maximum exposure. The whole campaign cost an estimated $500,000.

The advertising campaign in itself was huge. Full page advertisements were printed in America's leading newspapers and magazines. Large cardboard displays were erected throughout all record shops. Regular advertisements promoting ABBA's latest single 'Take A Chance On Me' were broadcast on national TV and radio. Perhaps the most extravagant advertisement was a giant and magnificent billboard that was strategically positioned overlooking Sunset Strip in Los Angeles.

The highlight of ABBA's visit came when they appeared as special guests on a national Olivia Newton-John TV Special. Olivia had first met ABBA when she was a fellow contestant in the 1974 Eurovision Song Contest. Since then Olivia's career had also rocketed and she was now an international superstar. In America, Olivia's record successes, together with the starring role in the record-breaking film Grease, had gained her tremendous popularity. To be Olivia's guests on her own television special meant that ABBA would be seen and heard by over thirty million American viewers.

"The whole thing was a beautiful experience" said Benny. "It was one of the best shows we've ever done. Olivia was a very lovely, warm person, and we all had a lot of fun doing the programme. Of course, we've done the usual quota of TV talk shows in America, but this one with Olivia was an important step for us. Besides presenting our music for large audiences of thirty to forty million viewers, we all sat down for a ten minute 'rap' session which gave the whole thing more intimacy."

It was during the 'rap' session that ABBA joined Olivia in singing The Beach Boys hit 'Barbara Anne'. Frida also delighted everyone when she sang some 'opera' publically for the first time. After ten days of solid promotion, ABBA left America knowing that 'ABBA month' was off to a great start.

Before returning to Stockholm ABBA visited Dusseldorf in Germany, where they appeared on The Star Parade Show and performed 'Eagle', 'Thank You For The Music' and 'Take A Chance On Me' live. Also appearing on the same show were America's most successful duo, The Carpenters, who were also currently involved with some heavy promotion throughout Europe. Back home in Sweden, there was much to do before Agnetha, Benny, Bjorn and Frida could begin to look forward to their first 'real' holiday in many years. One year of design and construction work was finally completed and during, the second half of May, ABBA's own recording studio was officially opened. Polar Music Studios was now ready to serve its creators – ABBA. At the official opening ceremony a very proud Benny said "It really is the most fantastic place, the most modern studio in the world. It has many facilities that you cannot find in any other studio anywhere else." Of course, Polar Studios was primarily for Agnetha, Benny, Bjorn and Frida's solid use. However, when they were not in residence, it would be made available for other artists and musicians. Already Led Zeppelin and Genesis were scheduled to record there. It was also during May that initial discussions took place with regard to ABBA's next world tour. "It look very likely that we will be touring in the spring or summer next year, but nothing has been actually fixed yet so that's all I'd better say" revealed Agnetha.

On June 12th the millionth copy of 'The Album' was sold in England. It was bought by a Mrs. Bonner, who paid +255 for it, the money going towards the Reading Hospital Appeal Fund. On collecting her unique album, Mrs. Bonner was also presented with a signed telegram from ABBA. ABBA The Album was now certified triple platinum in England. By the middle of June, Benny and Bjorn had successfully completed six new songs for ABBA's new album. Therefore, with everthing up to date, now was the time for a holiday. For the next seven weeks Agnetha, Benny, Bjorn and Frida would be leaving all the pressures of superstardom behind them. In their search for sun, sea and tranquility, Benny and Frida visited the Island of St. John in The Virgin Islands whilst Agnetha, Bjorn and children opted for the Caribbean. In late July, after returning home to Sweden, the holidays continued. Benny and Frida took to the seas and sailed their new boat along the Baltic Coast whilst Agnetha, Bjorn and children isolated themselves on their 'secret' island. Whilst Agnetha, Benny, Bjorn and Frida were enjoying their holidays the great success of 'ABBA month' became evident.

On July 20th, ABBA's Greatest Hits album was certified platinum after achieving one million American sales. Three weeks later, on August 18th, a double achievement followed – ABBA The Album was also certified platinum and 'Take A Chance On Me' peaked at number three on the American charts. With sales exceeding one million copies, 'Take A Chance On Me' was certified gold.

After their much-needed holiday, the second week of August saw ABBA back at work. Benny and Bjorn immediately took up residence at their new studio, where they began preparing the new songs, ready for Agnetha and Frida's vocals. Agnetha and Frida once again took charge of the visual responsibilities and began choosing costumes and photographs for future promotional purposes. It was also during August that Agnetha's own songwriting talents were honoured. 'The Swedish Society of Popular Music Composers' presented Agnetha with an award for her past solo compositions. During the first week of September Agnetha and Frida joined Benny and Bjorn in the studio to begin recroding vocals for the new album. In the meantime, on September 8th, an unexpected new ABBA single was released call 'Summer Night City'. "Before we went on holiday, we had no thoughts of putting out a single so far in front of the album" revealed Agnetha, "However, in the weeks we've been back, we've been listening to the six tracks now completed and felt that, since they were ready, we might just as well not keep all of them to ourselves – so we have a new single." The release of 'Summer Night City' took many by

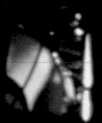

surprise, especially the critics, who seemed to be alarmed that ABBA should release a song with such a blatent disco sound. When asked, 'Why release a song that is powered by an unmistakable disco beat?", Bjorn replied, "Why not? Everyone's doing it, it's the pulse of the Seventies". Even so, the critics seemed less than impressed. "ABBA go disco, the songs is by no means as memorable as earlier stuff" wrote N.M.E., whilst Record Mirror said "The calculating Swedes have produced a piece of disco muzak." Melody Maker, who seemed to think that ABBA were being influenced by the Bee Gees, commented "It was only a matter of time before they sidled into the Gibb Brothers' disco penthouse."

As ABBA were busy working in the studios, 'Summer Night City' was promoted, once again, by an accompanying promotional video, which featured ABBA on land and water around the city of Stockholm. Despite being very different from all previous ABBA singles, 'Summer Night City' was still a big hit with fans around the world. By reaching number one in Sweden, Denmark, New Zealand, Luxembourg, number two in Finland, Austria, number three in France, Holland, Germany, Switzerland and number five in England, it showed that ABBA's audience were willing to grow with them.

The B-side brought to light a medley of three songs that ABBA had recorded in 1975. They were all traditional folk songs, 'Pick A Bale Of Cotton' and 'Midnight Special', featuring the combined vocals of Agnetha and Frida, together with the ballad, 'On Top Of Old Smokey', which was sung by Frida.

On October 6th ABBA took a day off from the recording studio, and celebrated. The occasion? Not more awards or records successes, but something rather more personal. Amid great secrecy, Benny and Frida were finally married at their local church in Lidingo, after spending nine years living together. The ceremony was so secret that even experienced journalists and press photographers were totally unaware of the happy occasion. "It had to be a quiet ceremony" said Benny afterwards, "We didn't want it to be like Bjorn and Agnetha's wedding where there were so many people it was just too crowded. Not that we didn't want our fans to know about it, but we both felt that our wedding was very personal, and we didn't was it spoiled by anything."

It was also during October that 'ABBA The Album' was certified gold in France and so ABBA seized the opportunity to go to Paris and collect their latest award. Whilst in Paris, ABBA were happy to accept the offer of singing their new single live on French television. As November arried ABBA found themselves travelling once again. Firstly, it was back to America, where they appeared on the Dick Clark show in Los Angeles, and then it was on to somewhere new – Japan. ABBA's immense popularity throughout Japan became evident to them upon their arrival in Tokyo – no fewer than three of their albums were currently occupying high positions on the Japanese album charts.

During their visit ABBA gave several press conferences and made various appearances on television. During one television appearance ABBA gave their Japanese audiences an exclusive hearing of two new songs from their forthcoming album, 'If It Wasn't For The Nights' and 'The King Has Lost His Crown'. The majority of ABBA's time was spent recording an hour-long television special for the Tokyo Broadcasting System, which was to be screened exclusively throughout Japan in December. ABBA returned to Sweden towards the end of November, but only had a few days' rest before their travels continued. This time the destination was England.

On Decmeber 7th, ABBA arrived in London for three days to film guest appearances for the 'Mike Yarwood Christmas Special' and 'The Jim'll Fix It Christmas Special'. For the 'Mike Yarwood Show', ABBA performed 'Thank You For The Music' together with a new song, 'If It Wasn't For The Nights', before a live and very enthusiastic studio audience. For the 'Jim'll Fix It Show', ABBA were filmed meeting two ABBA fans who were among over 50,000 people who had written to the BBC, all asking to meet them.

It was also whilst ABBA were in London that they announced their plans to participate in a forthcoming charity concert, to be held in New York in January, for the charity UNICEF (United Nations Children Fund). With the forthcoming Christmas Holidays fast approaching, it became clear that ABBA's new album would not appear until the following year, as Bjorn said, "The new album is nowhere near completion, unfortunately. We are going to have to think up at least six more songs before we have enough material to fill up both sides."

"The new album is nowhere near completion, unfortunately. We are going to have to think up at least six more songs before we have enough material to fill up both sides."

Nevertheless, ABBA would at least be seen over the Christmas period, as their appearances on numerous television shows would be screened. In that repsect ABBA were ending the year with the high profile with which they had started the year.

CHAPTER SIXTEEN
THE SHOW GOES ON

1979 began with the sad and totally unexpected news that Agnetha and Bjorn were seeking a divorce after eight years of marriage. Unbeknown to the public, Agnetha and Bjorn had been experiencing difficulties with their personal relationship for some time. Despite making every effort to resolve their differences, Agnetha and Bjorn found that they could not. Therefore, when Bjorn moved out of the family home of Christmas Eve, both he and Agnetha were mutually agreed that divorce was the best and only option left to take. "The break-up had been coming for quite a long time" said Agnetha, "We just drifted apart, it's as simple as that. When you talk about everything and you still don't get through to one another, then it's a sign that there's really nothing left between you. I guess we would have separated whether we were pop singers or not, and we would have made the same decision, if it had meant disbanding ABBA."

However, there was no question that Agnetha and Bjorn's divorce would affect ABBA in any way, and both were quick to stress that they would carry on working together professionally even though they were no longer partners in marriage. "ABBA have become stronger than ever before. We now have a purely professional relationship and all the difficult undertones have gone" said Bjorn.

Agnetha and Bjorn realised that news of their divorce would generate enormous interest and speculation from the world press. Therefore, in order to set the record straight, once and for all, Agnetha and Bjorn gave the facts to one Swedish newspaper.

AGNETHA- "Bjorn and I made the decision together and things are much better. Yes, I went through a period of unhappiness. Bjorn and I decided that together we'd consult a phychiastrist. We wanted an outside person looking at us, in case it should have been something abour our relationship that we both couldn't see. It didn' help to keep us together, but it did help us. We were told that the decision that we had already made – that we couldn't go on living together – was a good one. It wasn't easy to do but I feel very strong now. Our decision is a good one because we both agreed. If one meets another person and leaves because of that, it's a different situation, a sad one. I'm in a new phase now and it's quite exciting. It's much better now – much. Bjorn is still a good friend of min. You don't live with someone for eight years, have two children and not retain some feeling. All I can say is that the music had nothing to do with the split in our marriage."

BJORN – "Agnetha and I are both concerned about the welfare of the children, and we'll always be good friends. Agnetha and I have each bought a house about five minutes apart because our children are of the utmost importance to us. It is essential that they grow up able to see both their parents when they want to. It would be hopeless to live hundreds of miles apart. Agnetha and I have no problems working together now. Before we got the divorce we found that despite our best efforts at working things out, we found ourselves growing apart and our problems increasing. But we didn't give up on this marriage easily or quickly. It took two years before we finally agreed to end it. There was no tension, but of course there was much crying."

"I'd come to realise that Agnetha and I are totally different people. We were making our lives and the lives of everyone around us miserable. Once we'd made the decision to part, it eased a lot of tension in the group. The split had to come. It was a case of a parting of two egocentrics."

Despite Agnetha and Bjorn's insistance that their divorce was a mutual, personal decision, that would in now ay affect their professional relationship, inevitably very many newspapers and magazines reported rumours, inaccuracies and lies with much sensationalism.

For their part, Agnetha and Bjorn had done all that they could to dispel such rumours and so now was the time to show the world that as member of ABBA, Agnetha and Bjorn were very much united. On January 8th ABBA arrived in New York to take part in a charity concert which would launch 1979 as The Year Of The Child. Arranged by UNICEF (United Nations Children's Fund), the 'Gift of Song' concert was, in the words of United Nations Secretary General, Kurt Waldheim ". . .A concert with a purpose, designed to provide food, health care, shelter and eduction for the children in greatest

need in one hundred developing countries around the globe."
On Janaury 9th the 'Gift of Song' concert took place at the General Assembly Hall of the United Nations. Before a capacity audience and estimated television viewers totalling three hundred million from seventy different countries ABBA, together with Earth Wind and Fire, Andy Gibb, Donna Summer, Olivia Newton-John, Rod Stewart, John Denver, Kris Kristofferson, Rita Coulidge and The Bee Gees, all performed and donated the copyright of one song to UNICEF's 'Year of the Child' appeal. ABBA's 'Gift of Song' was a new track called 'Chiquitita' which, rather appropriately, was the Spanish translation of 'little girl'.

The estimated amount of money that the 'Gift of Song' concert was hoping to raise through the concert itself and through subsequent record sales, was 50,000,000+.

Immediately after the concert Agnetha and Frida returned to Sweden, whilst Benny and Bjorn went in search of sunshine and tranquility in order to write some new songs. They found all the inspiration they needed in Nassau, The West Indies, and during their stay wrote three new songs.

Before returning to Sweden, Benny and Bjorn spent a further week at Criteria recording studios in Maimi, where they recorded the backing track to a new song titled 'Voulez Vous'.

Back home in Sweden, Frida continued with her singing and dancing lessons, whilst Agnetha decided to escape all the current media attention regarding her and Bjorn's divorce, which promted Polar Music to release the following statement to the world press on January 19th, "Re: Bjorn and Agnetha. There will be no change as far as ABBA as a group is concerned, all our plans will continue as before. In middle of February ABBA will go to Switzerland to record a TV Special called 'Snowtime Special'. ABBA are hosts for this programme and there will be guest artists.

ABBA and the guest stars are donating all their fee and all the income from sales of this programme to UNICEF and 'The Year Of The Child'. The LP will probably be released in the middle of April, no name decided yet. There will maybe be a world tour, beginning in August. Best Regards, Polar Music."

On January 26th ABBA released 'Chiquitita' as their new single. After making an immediate impact throughout the world charts, it soon reached the number one position in Australia, New Zealand, France, Germany, Austria, Switzerland, Holland, Denmark, Sweden, Finland, Luxemburg, Israel and The West Indies. In England it peaked at number two. With 'Chiquitita' ABBA performed a group first and recorded it wih Spanish lyrics. The release of 'Chiquitita en Espnaol' firmly cemented ABBA's popularity throughout the Spanish-speaking territories, where it sold a record-breaking two and a half million copies. More importantly however, with ABBA donating all their royalties from the song to UNICEF's 'Year Of The Child', sales of both versions made a substantial contribution to the charity funds. The B-side to 'Chiquitita' was also a new song titled 'Lovelight', which had been recorded in the Autumn of 1978.

"ABBA, together with Earth Wind and Fire, Andy Gibb, Donna Summer, Olivia Newton-John, Rod Stewart, John Denver, Kris Kristofferson, Rita Coulidge and The Bee Gees, all performed and donated the copyright of one song to UNICEF's 'Year of the Child' Appeal."

The beginning of February saw ABBA back at Polar Studios in Stockholm, where the worked on their forthcoming album. Whilst ABBA were locked away in the studio, Stig travelled to Cannes, France to attend Midem, the international music business convention. Here Stig announced to the world press that ABBA would be embarking on their second world tour later in the year. The tour would not only take in Europe, but would include extensive dates throughout Canada and North America. Stig also hinted that the tour might also include dates in Japan where, in December alone, 800,000 records had been sold after ABBA's recent promotional visit there. Stig also announced that, after negotiatons with the authorities in Russia, they had agreed to release 'ABBA Arrival' and 'ABBA The Album' officially, instead of importing limited copies from other countries.

On February 14th ABBA travelled to Leysin, in Switzerland, where they were to make an hour long TV special for the BBC's 'Snowtime Special' series. This, the latest in the series, was to be aptly called 'ABBA In Switzerland'. Due to a mechanical problem which resulted in the plane carrying ABBA having to return, mid-flight to Stockholm's Arlanda Airport, ABBA's arrival in Leysin was somewhat behind schedule. When ABBA finally reached their destination in late afternoon, therefore, they were required to commence filming immediately.

ABBA's base for the next few days was the Central Hotel in Leysin, and it was here that they held a press conference at 7pm that same evening. The proceedings were started with ABBA being presented with gold disc awards for their latest chart success in England, 'Chiquitita'. Then it was question time . . . "Why do you choose various TV shows to make your rare appearances?', to which Bjorn replied "We did the UNICEF show in New York partly because it was for a very good cause but also because it was being broadcast everywhere in the world. It is the same for the Special we are doing here, right now. It is a good way of doing things. We still go to England and Germany to do promotions, but not so often now".

Next came questions regarding ABBA's next album. "We are writing and recording the album now and we will be finished around the beginning of April", said Benny. Then came the inevitable question with regard to Agnetha and Bjorn's recent divorce. "We don't wish to discuss our private lives with anybody. We have talked to one paper just to get things straight. We don't want to discuss it any more, at least not I", said Agnetha. Bjorn was a little more forthcoming. "Well, as you can see, we are good friends. There is no question, it is working really well and the divorce was because we couldn't live together, that's all. Everything is going really well with ABBA."

It was also at the press conference that Frida revealed that she would soon be realising one of her ambitions. Frida had accepted her first film role in a Swedish movie called 'Walk On Water If You Can', written and directed by two fellow Swedes, Stig Bjorkman and Sun Axelson. Not wanting to fall even further behind schedule, immediately after the press conference the BBC whisked ABBA off to the local ice skating rink where they filmed some more sequences for the TV special. Finally, at 11pm, ABBA were free to relax back at their hotel after one of their more chaotic days.

The following day ABBA made the twenty-minute journey to the neighbouring town of Les Diablerettes, where the day's activities consisted of photo sessions, interviews and more filming on and around the picturesque ski-slopes.

Day three, and the final day of filming, centred around the giant marquee that the BBC had erected in Leysin. This was the venue for the highlight of the TV special – ABBA performing a selection of old and new songs before 2,500 local citizens. In total ABBA performed seven songs which were separated by guest performances by Roxy Music and Kate Bush. From the seven songs ABBA performed, four were tracks from their forthcoming album, 'Chiquitita', 'The Kings Has Lost His Crown', 'Kisses Of Fire' and 'Does Your Mother Know'. With all filming now successfully completed, ABBA spent a further two days in Leysin relaxing and enjoying the ski-slopes in peace and quiet and away from the camera lens. Back home in Sweden, ABBA returned to the studio to add the final touches to their new album. Finally, by the beginning of April, the album was complete, leaving ABBA free to enjoy the forthcoming Easter holidays.

On Easter Sunday ABBA In Switzerland was screened throughout many European countries. Being ABBA's first TV special for some time, it had been eagerly anticipated by fans and critics alike. for once, the critics seemed to have enjoyed the show as much as the fans. "ABBA In Switzerland made staying at home in front of the box a real pleasure" wrote one critic, whose words summed up fellow-critics' general opinion of the show.

On April 27th ABBA provided the world with another preview of their forthcoming album in the form of their new single 'Does Your Mother Know'/'Kisses Of Fire'. Featuring Bjorn as lead vocalist, 'Does Your Mother Know' showed yet again ABBA's ability to produce first class disco-orientated music. Reaching number one in New Zealand, Germany, Austria, Finland and Luxembourg, and top five positions elsewhere, "Does your Mother Know' became ABBA's second hit single of the year.

The following week, on May 4th, ABBA released their new album in its entirety. Titled 'Voulez Vous', the album contained ten songs: 'As Good As New', 'Voules Vous', 'I Have A Dream', 'Angeleyes', 'The King Has Lost His Crown', 'If It Wasn't For The Nights', 'Chiquitita', 'Lovers (Live A Little Longer)', and 'Kisses of Fire'. Advance orders around the world were phenomenal, with 'Voulez Vous' achieving platinum status in England, Germany, Sweden, Australia, New Zealand and Japan during its first week of release.

As 'Voulez Vous' firmly embedded itself at the top of the world's charts, the critics began expressing their views of ABBA's latest product. For the first time since ABBA's rise to 'superstardom', the critics seemed to be unanimous in declaring Voulez Vous ABBA's strongest album to date. Both lyrically and musically, ABBA's progression was considerable and very few could find fault with this review by an American critic: "This LP should cement ABBA's American popularity, which was established through last year's platinum, 'The Album'. Mining the rich vein of 'Europop', which the band has almost invented and polished to perfection, ABBA uses a mixture of American rock funkiness, disco's slick pervasiveness, European pop sentiments, and a dose of universal sex appeal to create a package appealing to a broad demographic. With a heavy emphasis on the group's charming vocal harmonies, this LP is not so much an advance, as a culmination of ABBA's previous musical achievements."

The last week of May saw ABBA travel to Madrid, Spain where they recorded a TV special for their Spanish-speaking audiences. By now ABBA's Spanish version of 'Chiquitita' had sold a record-breaking two and a half million copies, and had topped the charts in Spain, Argentina, Peru, Panama, Columbia, Chile, Venezuela, Equador and El Salvador. This immense success had resulted in ABBA being firmly declared 'top pop group' throughout Spain and South America. Called 'Three Thousand Miles', the TV special enabled ABBA to peform a string of their most successful hits, together with the Spanish version of 'Chiquitita'.

As Agnetha, Benny and Bjorn returned to Sweden, Frida remained in Spain to begin filming her role in her first film, 'Walk On Water If You Can'. Filmed on location in Seville, the story centrered aound Orlando (Lena Nyman), who is a student at the University of Stockholm. Orlanda meets and falls in love with a Swedish diplomat from Argentina, played by Thomas Ponten. When Orlanda arrived in Argentina to see her newly-found love, she soon discovers that he is already married. Frida plays the part of the wife. Of her first film role, Frida said, "I was very pleased to appear in a truly dramatic film. When I heard that the film was being produced by the Swedish Film Institute, I asked for a part. I enjoyed the break from ABBA, but I'd never forsake the group for a film career."

Back home in Sweden, Benny and Bjorn were keen to get back to the studio. "We've had some great ideas for new numbers recently and we are impatient to get them down on tape. We are so pleased with them that we think they'll make good singles for the autumn. Once we have finished them, we will take a break" said Benny. During July ABBA did take a break. Benny and Frida sailed their board along the Baltic coast, Bjorn spent some time with this girlfriend, Lena Kallersjo, and Agnetha occupied herself with Linda and Christian.

On July 6th, ABBA released a double A-sided new single, 'Kisses of Fire'/'Voulez Vous'. Despite both tracks' inclusion on the now multi-million selling 'Voulez Vous' album, ABBA soon found themselves with another worldwide hit single. The last week of July and the whole of August saw ABBA back in Stockholm, rehearsing for their forthcoming world tour. Although the choreography would be very much improvised by Agnetha and Frida throughout the tour, ABBA needed to rehearse thoroughly all twenty-five songs included within their repertoire.

"I enjoyed the break from ABBA but I'd never forsake the group for a film career."

On September 5th, as the start of their world tour grew closer, ABBA spent the day in the studio, recording the vocals for a new song called 'Gimmie, Gimmie, Gimmie (A Man After Midnight).' This would be released as ABBA's new single whilst they were on tour. The accompanying promotional video, filmed by Lasse Hallstrom that same day, showed ABBA in the studio recording 'Gimmie, Gimmie, Gimmie' and provided fans the world over with an interesting insight of ABBA at work in their studio. After a week's rest the time had arrived for ABBA to forget recording studios and to concentrate on reproducing their music before live audiences . . .

CHAPTER SEVENTEEN
NORTH AMERICAN
& EUROPEAN TOUR

ITINERARY

13.9.79 - CANADA	- EDMONTON	- EDMONTON SPORTS ARENA
15.9.79 - CANADA	- VANCOUVER	- P.N.E.
17.9.79 - U.S.A.	- SEATTLE	- SEATTLE ARENA
18.9.79 - U.S.A.	- PORTLAND	- PORTLAND OPERA HOUSE
19.9.79 - U.S.A.	- CONCORD	- CONCORD PAVILLION
21.9.79 - U.S.A.	- LOS ANGELES	- ANAHEIM CONVENTION CENTER
22.9.79 - U.S.A.	- SAN DIEGO	- SAN DIEGO SPORTS ARENA
23.9.79 - U.S.A.	- TEMPE	- THE ACTIVE CENTER
24.9.79 - U.S.A.	- LAS VEGAS	- PERFORMING ARTS THEATRE,
26.9.79 - U.S.A.	- OMAHA	- CIVIC AUDITORIUM
27.9.79 - U.S.A.	- MINNEAPOLIS	- ST. PAUL CIVIC
29.9.79 - U.S.A.	- MILWAUKEE	- AUDITORIUM
30.9.79 - U.S.A.	- CHICAGO	- AUDITORIUM THEATRE
2.10.79 - U.S.A.	- NEW YORK	- RADIO CITY MUSIC HALL
3.10.79 - U.S.A.	- BOSTON	- MUSIC HALL
4.10.79 - U.S.A.	- WASHINGTON DC	- CONSTITUTION HALL
6.10.79 - U.S.A.	- MONTREAL	- FORUM
7.10.79 - CANADA	- TORONTO	- MAPLE LEAF GARDENS

12 DAY BREAK

19.10.79 - SWEDEN	- GOTHENBURG	- SCANDAVAVIUM
20.10.79 - SWEDEN	- STOCKHOLM	- ISSTADION
21.10.79 - DENMARK	- COPENHAGEN	- FALKONER THEATRE
23.10.79 - FRANCE	- PARIS	- PAVILLION de PARIS
24.10.79 - HOLLAND	- ROTTERDAM	- AHOY SPORTPALEIS
25.10.79 - GERMANY	- DORTMUND	- WESTFALEHALLE
27.10.79 - GERMANY	- MUNCHEN	- OLYMPIAHALLE
28.10.79 - SWITZERLAND	- ZURICH	- HALLENSTADION
29.10.79 - GERMANY	- WEIN	- STADTHALLE
30.10.79 - GERMANY	- STUTTGART	- SPORTHALLE BOEGLINGEN
1.11.79 - GERMANY	- BREMEN	- STADTHALLE
2.11.79 - GERMANY	- FRANKFURT	- FESTHALLE
3.11.79 - BELGIUM	- BRUSSELS	- FOREST NATIONAL
5.11.79 - ENGLAND	- LONDON	- WEMBLEY ARENA
6.11.79 - ENGLAND	- LONDON	- WEMBLEY ARENA
7.11.79 - ENGLAND	- LONDON	- WEMBLEY ARENA
8.11.79 - ENGLAND	- LONDON	- WEMBLEY ARENA
9.11.79 - ENGLAND	- LONDON	- WEMBLEY ARENA
10.11.79 - ENGLAND	- LONDON	- WEMBLEY ARENA
11.11.79 - ENGLAND	- STAFFORD	- BINGLEY HALL
12.11.79 - ENGLAND	- STAFFORD	- BINGLEY HALL
13.11.79 - SCOTLAND	- GLASGOW	- APOLLO THEATRE
15.11.79 - IRELAND	- DUBLIN	- R.D.S. MAIN HALL

Through hard work and determination, ABBA's popularity throughout America and Canada was now evident. It was therefore with much excitement and anticiaption that ABBA looked forward to their first-even life performances before American and Canadian audiences: "From the beginning we said that we did not want to tour the U.S. as a supporting act for anyone else – we wanted to be the headliners" said Benny, and it was as headliners that ABBA arrived in Edmonton, Canada on Tuesday 11th September for the start of their first North American Tour.

After spending a full day rehearsing for the final time on September 13th, everything was in order for ABBA's premiere performance in Canada. ABBA held a press conference at their hotel before travelling the short distance to their first venue, The Edmonton Sports Arena. By 7pm a capacity audience of 14,000 had gathered and eagerly awaited ABBA's appearance on stage. Backstage, Agnetha, Benny, Bjorn and Frida were experiencing pre-show nerves, but as soon as they appeared on the smoke-covered stage, the audience greeted them with a deafening roar of approval, and all nerves disappeared.

Dressed in white, purple and blue sking-tight costumers, ABBA thrilled the audience with niney minutes of non-stop music. In total ABBA performed twenty-four songs, three of which were solo performances. Frida performed an energetic version of 'Why Did It Have To Be Me'. Benny amazed everyone with his instrumental 'Intermezzo No 1' and Agnetha stunned everyone with a self-written ballad called 'I'm Still Alive'. When it came to the final three songs, 'Dancing Queen', 'The Way Old Friends Do' and 'Waterloo', the audience were left captivated by ABBA's outstanding performance. Relieved that their debut concert had been a resounding success, back at their hotel ABBA held a celebratory party that lasted well into the early hours of the morning.

The following morning the first and perhaps, for once, the all-important reviews were read. All were extremely positive and undoubtedly gave ABBA a welcome burst of encouragement. "Swedish rock/pop group ABBA, doing their first North American tour, in a show that uncompromisingly demonstrated they are as good in person as they are on records." "Two dozen of their catchiest tunes were jammed into a 90 minute blockbuster of a show." ". . . a refreshing change from the standard rock concert, alive and full of positive energy". "One thing is for certain – the ABBA explosion is just beginning in the U.S." On Friday afternoon ABBA travelled to Vancouver, where on Saturday they performed to their biggest audience of the tour – 17,000 people. On Monday the tour proceeded to America, and it was in Seattle that ABBA met their American audience for the first time. Once again, all pre-show nerves soon disappeared when the American audience greeted ABBA with the same deafening roar of approval that the Canadian audiences had given them.

To celebrate ABBA's successful American debut, Atlantic Records held a celebratory after-show party for them at their hotel. Here the happy and relaxed atmosphere was enjoyed by all. In San Fransisco ABBA played the only open air concert of the tour at the Concord Pavillion, which led Benny to remark "This will be like being at the Folkparks again". After this concert Benny and Bjorn spoke to journalists and told them how happy and amazed they were at how the audiences had responded to ABBA. "When 8000 people in San Fransisco are standing up, clapping to music we wrote years ago – it's a wonderful feeling", said Benny.

CHAPTER EIGHTEEN
THE DREAM LIVES ON

Whilst ABBA occupied themselves with their world tour, their attack on the world's charts continued. On October 12th 'Gimmie Gimmie Gimmie (A Man After Midnight)' was released as ABBA's new single. Once again, ABBA's great command of producing disco-orientated music was evident and 'Gimmie Gimmie Gimmie' soon made a big impact on the world's charts.

Within weeks of its release 'Gimmie Gimmie Gimmie' was riding high at the top of the charts in Austria, Finland, Switzerland, Israel, Holland, Denmark, Sweden and New Zealand. In France, Belgium and Luxembourg it reached number two, whilst in England and Germany 'Gimmie Gimmie Gimmie' peaked at number three.

Two weeks later, on November 2nd, ABBA's second greatest hits compilation album was released. 'Greatest Hits Volume 2' brought ABBA's domination of the world charts during the Seventies up-to-date, and contained fourteen songs: 'Gimmie Gimmie Gimmie', 'Knowing Me Knowing You', 'Take A Chance On Me', 'Money Money Money', 'Rock Me', 'Eagle', 'Angel Eyes', 'Dancing Queen', 'Does Your Mother Know', 'Chiquitita', 'Summer Night City', 'I Wonder (Departure)', 'The Name Of The Game' and 'Thank You For The Music'.

Despite every track being a million seller in its own right, 'Greatest Hits Volume 2' gave ABBA their second hit album of the year. In England alone 600,000 copies were sold during its first week of release, resulting in 'Greatest Hits Volume 2' entering England's album chart at number one. The same story was told elsewhere.

On December 7th ABBA released their final single of the seventies, 'I Have A Dream' together with a live version of 'Take A Chance On Me', which was recorded at London's Wembley Arena in November. Released as a souvenir collector's item, so that ABBA could say "Thank You" to all their fans who had supported them throughout their recent world tour, 'I Have A Dream' became ABBA's final hit single of the decade, by reaching number one in France, Holland, Switzerland, Israel and Luxembourg, number two in England, New Zealand and Finland, and number four in Germany.

It was also during December that Stig, on ABBA's behalf, accepted a whole array of gold, double gold and platinum disc awards for ABBA's record sales in India, Austria, Portugal, Hong Kong, Nigeria, Switzerland, Kenya and Germany. Two further awards also came from America. Cashbox magazine which, in their annual summing up of the international music scene, declared ABBA 'No 1 International Mixed Group-Pop' and 'No. 1 International Group-Pop'.

As people around the world looked forward to a new decade, they also celebrated the end of an era – the seventies, that musically most certainly belonged to ABBA.

CHAPTER NINETEEN
ON AND ON AND ON

As the New Year and new decade began, ABBA were fully refreshed and immediately returned to work. Due to the previous six month's touring commitments, Benny and Bjorn had suffered a creative 'dry-spell'; therefore, they now desparately needed to begin writing new songs for the next ABBA album. In their search for some peace, tranquility, inspiration and warm weather, Benny and Bjorn spent January composing in Florida. Whilst Benny and Bjorn were busy creating new ABBA songs, back home in Stockholm, Agnetha and Frida were equally busy, recreating a selection of 'old' ABBA songs.

In view of the tremendous success the Spanish version of 'Chiquitita' had achieved throughout the Spanish-speaking territories, it was decided to release a full album of ABBA's best know songs complete with Spanish lyrics. So during January Agnetha and Frida took up residence at Polar Studios and re-recorded the vocals, in Spanish, to the following ABBA songs: 'Thank-You For The Music', 'Dancing Queen', 'Move On', 'Gimmie Gimmie Gimmie', 'Fernando', 'I Have A Dream', 'Mamma Mia', 'Hasta Manana' and 'Knowing Me Knowing You'. During the frist week of February, Benny and Bjorn returned from their 'highly productive' stay in Florida and immediately joined Agnetha and Frida at Polar Studio to begin mixing the songs for their Spanish album.

JAPANESE TOUR

ITINERARY
March 12th	Tokyo
March 13th	Tokyo
March 14th	Koriyama
March 17th	Tokyo
March 18th	Tokyo
March 20th	Fukuoka
March 21st	Osaka
March 22nd	Osaka
March 24th	Nagoya
March 26th	Tokyo
March 27th	Tokyo

On Saturday March 8th ABBA tavelled to Japan for their first live performances before a Japanese audience. During their three week visit, ABBA performed eleven concerts throughout Japan, including six shows at the world-famous Budokan in Tokyo. Being an extension of the North American and European tour, the format of each concert remained the same as those throughout America and Europe. However, there was one inuque difference at each of the Japanese concerts. When it came to singing 'I Have A Dream', ABBA surprised and thrilled the audiences by singing it in Japanese! ABBA's first tour of Japan was an enormous success, and after performing for over 100,000 hysterical Japanese fans, ABBA returned to Sweden on March 29th.

With no more tours planned for the foreseeable future, back at home in Stockholm ABBA now concentrated on their forthcoming album and took up residence at Polar Studios. During May ABBA's 'Spanish Album', titled 'Gracias Por La Musica', was released in all Spanish-speaking territories. As predicted, the album was an immediate success and soon found its way to the top of the charts in Argentina, Chile, Columbia, Equador, El Salvador, Spain, Panama, Peru and Venezuela. To coincide with the release of 'Gracias Por La Musica', ABBA recorded a television special in which they performed a selection of the album's tracks.

During the last two weeks of June, Agnetha, Benny, Bjorn and Frida began their summer holidays, after successfully completing six new songs for the new ABBA album. This year all four decided to spend this summer in Sweden. Benny and Frida once again sailed their boat along the Baltic coast, Bjorn and his girlfriend, Lean, retreated to their island, whilst Agnetha stayed at her newly-bought summer house on the outskirts of Stockholm. On July 25th ABBA's first single of the Eighties was released, titled 'The Winner Takes It All'. Released together with a highly-acclaimed promotional video, the obvious lyrical and musical strength of 'The Winner Takes It All' resulted in ABBA's scoring their first hit of the new decade. Worldwide sales for the song were phenomenal, and within weeks had reached the number one position in no less than twenty-three different countries.

During the first week of August, Benny, Bjorn and Frida visited England. Primarily they were in London to attend Pink Floyd's 'The Wall' concert, but they also seized the opportunity to speak to several journalists. In an interview for The Sun newspaper Benny was asked if ABBA were bothered by the critics who described their music as bland and boring, to which Benny replied "Not any more. When millions of people all over the world buy our records. I think you know who is right and who is wrong. However, the only thing that annoys us is when we spend the best part of a year working on an album – just to get it right – then our hard work is attacked. That is very annoying."

With ABBA's latest album nearing completion, Benny was also asked about ABBA's future plans and wishes. he said "Financially, we no longer have any worries. And our dreams of superstardom have exceeded our wildest dreams. We like our musical results and as long as we do, we'll keep playing. We'll stop when it's no longer fun. We have realised all of our dreams, there is nothing we could ever wish for; however, we do need new goals and new ideas to keep us busy working."

"We have realised all of our dreams, there is nothing we could ever wish for; however, we do need new goals and new ideas to keep us busy working."

By the end of September ABBA's new album was finally complete and so ABBA immediately turned their attentions to promotional business. Using the theme of a circus to promote the album, ABBA's first task was to photograph the album sleeve and film the promotional video for their forthcoming single, to be taken from the album.

So during the first weekend of October ABBA, together with a group fo circus performers, took up residence at the Europa Film Studios in Stockholm, where all photo sessions and filming in connection with the new album were carried out.

On October 31st ABBA's new album, titled 'Super Trouper', was released. The album's ten songs: 'Super Trouper', 'The Winner Takes It All', 'On and On and On', 'Andante Andante', 'Me and I', 'Happy New Year', 'Our Last Summer', 'The Piper', 'Lay All Your Love On Me' and 'The Way Old Friends Do)' recorded live at Wembley Arena, London), were an immediate hit with fans and critics alike. "For unlike some of their contemporaries, ABBA make great pop songs that have magic – that ethereal quality which no critic can define, analyse or rationalise. 'The Winner Takes It All' is pehaps the supreme example of this magical ambiance. The final tracks, 'Lay All Your Love On Me' and 'The Way Old Friends Do', are more than just songs' – they're hymns", wrote Lynden Barber for Melody Maker, whilst Mike Gardner from Record Millor wrote "The secret to ABBA is never to hear them on an album where the highs become a level, but each track needs to be savoured amid the dross that most other musicians xerox out in the name of rock 'n' roll on the radio. Benny Andersson and Bjorn Ulvaeus are eft craftsmen whose ability to conjure up a memorable melody puts to shame most of these who dare to assume the mantle of tunesmiths". Many critics, however, only used a few words to express their opinion of ABBA's latest: "A wonderful album – their best yet"; "ABBA have surpassed themselves once again"; "Congratulations ABBA – the best you have done"; "Absolutely outstanding". In England, advance orders for 'Super Trouper' were a record-breaking one million copies. In one day alone it sold a phenomenal 160,000 copies, resulting in 'Super Trouper' topping the charts in England during its first week of release. Similar statistics were achieved elsewhere throughout the world, making 'Super Trouper' ABBA's biggest and fastest selling album to date. In the Spanish-speaking territories, the fans were given an added bonus, for two of the tracks, 'Andante Andante' and 'Happy New Year', were recorded in Spanish.

The following week, on November 7th, ABBA released 'Super Trouper' as their new single. Despite the phenomenal sales of 'Super Trouper' the album, the single was an immediate world-wide hit, and resulted in ABBA's topping both the album and single charts simultaneously in England, Finland, Australia, New Zealand, Austria, Switzerland, Israel, France, Germany, Denmark, Sweden, Holland, Luxembourg and Belgium.

As ABBA began talking to various journalists from around the world, it seemed that not one of them could find any fault with the 'Super Trouper' album. For once, it seemed that everyone was accepting 'Super Trouper' for what it was – an outstanding album from the world's leading pop group. "The criticism that we've had over the years, except on this album, is that we try to adjust our music to suit our audience. This is completely wrong because we are the only musicians in Sweden and one of the few in the world who can afford to do exactly what we want to do. Because we have all the time in the world. We have our own studio. We have money and we have status", said Benny.

During November, Agnetha, Benny, Bjorn and Frida took a short break from ABBA. For Agnetha and Bjorn this short break gave them the opportunity to fulfill some personal ambitions. Agnetha realised her wish to record an album together with her daughter, Linda. So during November Agnetha and Linda took up residence at Polar Studios and recorded a selection of eighteen traditional Christmas carols and children's songs, in Swedish. The album was also produced by Agnetha, together with Michael B. Tretow, and was to be released throughout Scandanavia the following year.

For Bjorn, his personal ambition became a reality when he travelled to Hawaii and took part in a marathon together with thousands of the world's top runners. ABBA had planned to visit England, France and Germany in December in order to record some television shows for the forthcoming Christmas period. However, due to a frightending and sick security threat, they had to drastically reconsider their plans. In early December a note was delivered, anonymously, to the Polar Music offices in Stockholm, threatening the safety of ABBA and their children. "Whoever's writing the notes said that if we went on tour, they'd hurt our children", said Agnetha.

Christer Koch, Stockholm's Police Chief, was assigned to investigate the threats, and told reporters "We are treating each threat as the serious matter it is. We're getting information but we cannot talk about it or give details." Despite being obviously upset and sickened by the threat, Bjorn said "You can't let your life be affected because there are maniacs out there. And while we're more conscious and more on the lookout to protect our children's safety, we refuse to be like Elvis Presley, renting a movie theatre in order to close it – just so that we can take our children to the movies. That is terribly sad."

However, until further police investigatiaons into the threats were carried out, Agnetha, Benny, Bjorn and Frida were advised to stay in Stockholm – and all ABBA's travel plans were regrettably cancelled. In Gemany, ABBA were due to record a television show called 'Show Express' in which they would have performed six songs from their 'Super Trouper' album, but because of the security threat it seemed certain that this, too, would have to be cancelled. But the German TV Company were so keen to broadcast the show during Christmas that they flew the technicians, film crew and stage set to Stockholm. This made it possible for ABBA to record the show as planned without having to leave Stockholm. As Agnetha and Bjorn looked forward to a happy and safe Christmas with their children, Benny and Frida fortunately did not have to cancel their planned Christmas skiiing holiday in Switzerland. As the year closed it was announced that the 'Super Trouper' album had already sold seven milliion copies worldwide, which undoubtedly confirmed that ABBA's phenomenal worldwide popularity had now transferred to the Eighties.

"You can't let your life be affected because there are maniacs out there. And while we're more conscious and more on the lookout to protect our children's safety, we refuse to be like Elvis Presley, renting a movie theatre in order to close it – just so that we can take our children to the movies. That is terribly sad."

CHAPTER TWENTY
FOUR-PART HARMONY

1981 began with celebrations and personal changes for Agnetha, Benny, Bjorn and Frida. The first celebration took place amid great secrecy at a church in Stockholm; on Sunday 14th January, Bjorn married his girlfriend, Lena.

The second celebration received far greater publicity and was a major event throughout Sweden. On January 25th, Stig celebrated his 50th birthday and a huge party was held at his house in Stockholm. Among the three hundred plus guests were, natually, Agnetha, Benny, Bjorn and Frida, who presented Stig with their own unique and special birthday present. The previous day, Saturday 24th, Agnetha, Benny, Bjorn and Frida had dressed themselves in their original Eurovision Song Contest costumes and were filmed at Berns Nightclub, in Stockholm, singing their unique birthday tribute to Stig. The song, specially written by Benny and Bjorn, called 'Hovas Vittne' (Happy Birthday), was then pressed onto 12 inch red vinyl and presented to Stig along with the accompanying video. Only two hundred copies of 'Hovas Vittne' were pressed, and today it still remains the rarest ABBA record in existence. The final week of January saw Benny and Bjorn travel to New York for a week's holiday to check out the latest musical developments in the U.S. Whilst there Benny and Bjorn went to see three muscials on Broadway, '42nd Street', 'Evita' and 'The Pirates of Penzance'. "Apart from those shows" said Bjorn, ". . . we mostly listened to the radio, watched television and saw a few sights. New York is a very exhilarating place and we weren't there on business so that made a change."

Upon their return to Sweden on February 10th, Benny and Bjorn began writing new material for the next ABBA ablum. "Initially we plan to write 3 or 4 new songs, out of which we will pick a single" said Bjorn. However, two days later Benny took a short break from writing to concentrate on a personal matter. On Thursday February 12th, Benny and Frida announced to the world's press that they were seeking a divorce, and issued this joint statement: "The decision has been taken after considerable consideration and mutual agreement. We realise there will now be speculation in the press but we shall have to accept that. Our private life is our own affair and has nothing to do with anyone else. This step won't affect our partnership in ABBA. It is of a completely private nature."

FRIDA – "Now that Benny and I have broken up, we're able to work together better. Our relationship is more calm and relaxed. Benny and I are good friends and we really do like each other. There is nothing sad about it. We've just grown apart because of our different interests in life. We've always been honest with one another. We talked and talked and talked and finally agreed that divorce was the only answer."

BENNY – "Frida and I still remain friends. What keeps us together now is that we respect each other for what we can do together musically. I don't know how other people deal with this. It's all new to me. Frida and I did discuss whether the group would be able to stay together after our break-up. We were very close to splitting for a while. But we figured that the group had weathered the break-up of Bjorn and Agnetha so they could handle ours as well. We decided to stick together for the sake of the music. After all, we do enjoy what we do."

Predictably, many newspapers and magazines reported the divorce of Benny and Frida with much sensationalism, and rumours that ABBA were to split up were widespread. In comparison, two publications, New Musical Express and Songwriter, published interesting interviews with Benny and Bjorn which dealt purely with ABBA's professional partnership.

N.M.E. – "Are you friends, you ABBA people?"

BENNY – "Yes we are. First and foremost I think. Each of us shows consideration for what the others think. That is incredibly important. Otherwise you can't keep it together. It's enough if one of us says: "I don't want to do that because . . ." And then the other three: "All right." And we won't do it. That is very good. We are in an extremely privileged position because we can choose. We are not dependent on it to survive."

"We decided to stick together for the sake of the music. After all, we do enjoy what we do."

N.M.E. – "Can you say in all honesty that you are making the type of music that satisfied you?"

BENNY – "Yes, I'll absolutely state that. There is nothing that grabs me as much as when I heard a good pop song for the first time."

SONGWRITER – "How do you start writing a song? What comes first and what comes last?"

BJORN – "Always the melody comes first. What we do sometimes is play old things – little things that we've kept through the years but haven't been able to put into other songs yet. We play these little things to see if this time something will come up to complete one of them. If it doesn't, we just go on playing different chord structures, different rhythms. We go on playing and playing and playing."

SONGWRITER – "Are you writing songs or records?"

BJORN – "Ninety-five percent we're writing songs. We know that it is going to be on record but it has to be a song to start with, not just something of which we think 'This is probably going to sound good in the studio, although it doesn't sound good now'. We always say that a good melody is something that you could sing with just a piano or guitar and people would hear it. If you can do that it makes things very much easier for you in the studio."

BENNY – "We've spent so many hours in the studio trying to do a song better than it actually is. We've learned to recognise situations like that. What we do nowadays is just drop it and let it be, and maybe sooner or later we can use it in another song. It's a waste of time getting stuck in the studio. If it's not there from the beginning, it's probably not going to come."

SONGWRITER – "Are you aiming at writing hits? Are you consciously trying to be commercial or is the creaton of 'art' your goal?"

BJORN – "A lot of people think that, since our hits have been so consistent through so many years, we know how to make a hit song from the beginning, which is wrong. We write until we feel, "Oh, this is a hell of a good song." Writing a new song gives us a tremendous kick. I would say it's probably the biggest kick during the process of recording of an album and I think that gets through to people listening."

BENNY – "We don't think about what a hit is when we're writing, but I recognise one when I hear one. It's the same mechanism if I hear somebody else's song. I know that it is something because I like it. That's the only criterion. We basically write a song that we're proud of, record it the best way we can, and release is because we think it's very good. If other people like it, that's fine. But I have no criterion that it should be or has to be art. It is related to art in that we're serious about it. It's essential to be serious, even if it doesn't sound serious. It sounds like fun, fun, fun all the time, but it isn't."

N.M.E. – "Are there things you regret, now that you have been able to look at them from a disatance?"

BENNY- "No, no regrets. But sometimes you say that you could have done certain records better. For example, we did a song not too long ago called 'Summer Night City' – that wasn't too good. Sometimes you get all tied up. That was a single we had to do. We only had that song to work with, did the mixing for a week and at the end got tired. We said, 'OK, we'll finish it, release it and begin the next one.' But it doesn't matter really. If what one did eight years ago were better than what one is doing now – that would be catastrophe."

SONGWRITER – "What happens when you go into the studio."

BJORN – "What happens is what develops; you drop a few things, you keep a few things, and the end product could be cemething that we never thought of before. In a way it's irrational. We're only listening for something that feels good."

BENNY – "We have a lot of fun when we record. The whole period of being in the studio is maybe eighty percent laughing. It's really a fantanstic feeling going in the studio when you know that you have some good songs and you know something good will come out of it. It's the kind of life I would wish for everybody. What we're doing probably shows in the result. There is always the chance that we will come up with something that nobody has ever heard. It's the feeling of being close to that that brings the enjoyment. But I don't know what I like the most – writing or actually recording and producing the record. It's all very integrated."

N.M.E. – " It all souns so easy for you. You are so satisfied and happy?"

BENNY – "Wouldn't you feel good if you were in my position? I Think you would."

N.M.E. – "Do you mean that?"

BENNY- "You know what you like. You know that you like to write music. You know that you like to write songs and play them. And that is what you do. And if you can do what makes you most satisfied and get success from it . . ."

N.M.E. – "Automatic happiness?"

BENNY – "No, but obviously it makes you satisfied with a hell of a lot in your existence. But it also depends on what sort of person you are. One can't say that everybody that has got success feels the same. But if you can do what you yourself want to do, then you stand a better chance of being happy than if you do what somebody else wants you to do."

SONGWRITER – "In what ways do you see yourself growing?"

BJORN – "We are writing more personally. There are several different explanations for that. I'm much freer now with the English language than I used to be. Also, we're grown-up people, not so afraid of sharing with others what we feel, sharing things that have happened to ourselves. The meaning is becoming more important, I write in English and I even think in English when I write the lyrics."

BENNY – "It's becoming more and more important to integrate personal feelings into it. I think that has more to do with age than anything else. There is something that happened between the 'Voulez Vous' and the 'Super Trouper' album, a definite development. I don't know if that shows, but I hear it. I think the next album will be even a little broader expression of what we're up to. It's great to know we still can open doors and both still have the will to continue and progress. That's a kick in itself which I hope will reflect on what we're doing also."

SONGWRITER – "If you could distill your work into one message to the world, what would it be? Do you see yourselves as a political force?"

BJORN – "The message would be that we're pleasing ourselves in exactly the same way as we hope to please those who listen to our music. In other words, that we share something that is absolutely honest. There's one song on the 'Super Trouper' album which is as close as we've come to writing something really political – 'Happy New Year'. I feel that one of the biggest problems in the Western world today is lack of confidence, and the way of looking negatively at the future. So the song is about trying to set up positive goals for the future. That's a political message in itself."

For the majority of March, April and May ABBA were busy at Polar Studios, working on their forthcoming album. However, on April 27th, 28th and 29th, ABBA moved from the recording studio to the television studio to make a '10 years with ABBA' TV Special.

The show was to include an interview with ABBA, followed by a live studio performance. American talk show host Dick Cavett was imported to conduct the interview and host the show, whilst ABBA's usual musicians provided the music for the live performance. "We wanted to do something really special" said Bjorn. "We've been together for more than ten years and yet a proper interview with all four of us at the same time, where people have the chance to get to know us in depth, has never been done. A very superficial picture of ABBA is most often spread."

During their live performance, ABBA performed a selection of their familiar songs and premiered two brand new numbers, 'Slipping Through My Fingers' and 'Two For The Price Of One'. During the interview ABBA talked freely about their years working together and also provided an insight into the background workings surrounding ABBA.

FRIDA – "What the public sees and hears is just a tiny fraction of all the time and effort we put into it. We rehearse each song endlessly and take the harder parts home for more practice. When we began rehearsing for this show, we had just been in the studio finishing a couple of songs for the new album. Rehearsals were held in the same place we had used on the eve of our 1979 world tour, with all the same musicians. Suddenly it felt as if there hadn't been any pause at all, that it was yesterday we last stood together on stage. It felt wonderful. Three days later we moved to the studio, tested the lights and sound and did all the songs all over and over again. Naturally you're tired after singing all day and perhaps you've sung the same song twenty times, but we set very high standards for ourselves. There is always something that can be a little better, but the resutls make it all worthwhile."

AGNETHA – "There's always a special atmosphere backstage, a nervous one. People are running back and forth calling to each other. It often feels like being at a circus. During the years I've learned how important it is to relax, to have a moment to yourself, before it's time to go on. Our children are often backstage when we perform. Mostly, we resemble a circus family. Everybody helps each other with clothes, make-up, hair styling, going for the coffee and so on. It provides security and a group feeling. You're part of something more than just four people who sing together. Worst of all are the minutes before you go on. You're made up, clothes in order, bursting with energy, but you can't take the stage. You have to wait for your cue.

BENNY – "I'm often struck by the thought of how unfair it is that all the praise always goes to those who stand in the spotlight. You must never forget the importance of the people who work backstage. When we do something big like a TV Special or a tour, we have an entire team of people who strive to see that everything goes as smoothly as possible for us. If everything is working, you can go out and give the audience your best. Just as important as their being skilled profesionals, is their being nice people. If the person doing my make-up is in a bad mood, I get in a bad mood myself. The people who create our clothes have to know our personalities in order to make the right things. When I stand at the front of the stage and receive the applause from the audience, I would like to give a part of that praise to everyone who has worked behind me."

In June, Agnetha, Benny, Bjorn and Frida began their summer holidays. Both Agnetha and Bjorn spent time with their children whilst Benny and Frida spent their first summer with their new partners. "Mona (Noeklit) is my new companion" said Benny, whilst Frida said "I've learned from my mistakes in the past. I don't want my new man facing all the publicity and questions, and that's why I'm keeping his name a secret. But you can tell everyone that I'm in love and Frida has a new fella."

In America, 'On and On and On' had now followed 'Lay All Your Love On Me' to reach the number one position on the Disco charts. These successes in America therefore inspired ABBA's record company in England to release both songs as a special 12-inch collector's item. When released on July 18th 'Lay All Your Love On Me' made an immediate impact on the charts and, within weeks, ABBA, made chart history in England. By reaching the number seven position, 'Lay All Your Love On Me'/'On And On And On' became the very first 12-inch-only release to achieve such a high position on England's charts. It was also at this time that ABBA were honoured by the American Guild of Variety Artists, who awarded them the title of 'Vocal Group of the Year 1981'.

Meanwhile, in Japan, a limited number of fans were treated to a brand new ABBA single release when 'Slipping Through My Fingers' was pressed on to a limited number of picture discs as part of a Japanese Coca-Cola promotional campaign. By August Benny and Bjorn had returned from their holidays and began writing the final songs for the new album. Meanwhile, Agnetha and Frida continued their holidays until the beginning of September, when they joined Benny and Bjorn at Polar Studios to begin recording.

On Saturday 12th September ABBA travelled to Bournemouth, England, where that evening they attended the annual CBS Sales Convention Dinner and Cocktail Evening at the Carlton Hotel. Here ABBA's attendance was greatly appreciated by the CBS sales representatives. "ABBA weren't remote or withdrawn like some stars" said John Mair, Head of CBS Sales. "One of the New York reps confided in me afterwards "Aren't they such lovely people?' ABBA really did us proud that evening and they have raised our morale no end."

The following day ABBA returned to Stockholm and continued recording their new album. However, on September 14th, Agnetha went to Majorca for a week's holiday with her sister. On her return she immediately rejoined Benny, Bjorn and Frida at Polar Studios. By November ABBA had successfully completed their new album and therefore occupied themselves with promotional activities. All promotional photographs in connection with the new album were taken against a backdrop of paintings at Julius Kronbergs Atelje, a public museum in Skansen, Stockholm. Promotional videos were filmed for three songs from the album 'One Of Us', 'When All is Said And Done' and 'Head Over Heels', all directed as usual by Lasse Hallstrom. Then ABBA concentrated on press and television interviews. In Stockholm the Foreign Press Association held a huge press conference for ABBA at which they spoke to journalists from all over the world including, Russia, Korea, Italy, U.S.A., Egypt, Spain, France, Germany and England.

On December 4th ABBA released their new single, 'One Of Us'/'Should I Laugh Or Cry'. Despite being the first new single release by ABBA for over a year, 'One Of Us' became an immediate worldwide success and, once again, placed ABBA at the top of the charts around the world. The following week, on 11th December, ABBA released their new album in its entirety.

Titled 'The Visitors', the album contained nine songs: 'The Visitors (Crackin' Up)', 'Head Over Heels', 'When All Is Said And Done', 'Soldiers', 'I Let The Music Speak', 'One Of Us', 'Two For The Price Of One', 'Slipping Through My Fingers' and 'Like An Angel Passing Through My Room'. Throughout all Spanish-speaking territories, 'When All is Said And Done' and 'Slipping Through My Fingers' were released with Spanish translations. Both musically and lyrically, 'The Visitors' was very different from all previous ABBA albums, on which many critics commented.

"'The Visitors' represents progress, and that is in the musical development of the group. 'The Visitors' and 'I Let The Music Speak' are both over five minutes long, marathons by ABBA standards."

129

'The Visitors' represents progress, and that is in the musical development of the group. 'The Visitors' and 'I Let The Music Speak' are both over five minutes long, marathons by ABBA standards. They are not padded, nor are they extended disco-cuts. Both lengthy tracks tell long tales and this in itself reflects great progress. Suddenly the songsters seem to have dined on dictionaries and thesauri. Of course, no ABBA album worth its money would contain fewer than two perfect pieces of pop production, and a worthy pair are present on 'The Visitors'. 'One Of Us' and 'Head Over Heels' are light and infectious delights" wrote Paul Gambaccini for the Express, whilst Bill Provick, from America's The Citizen, wrote "What had made ABBA such big business in the recording industry has been the exceptionally high quality of their product and the fact that their basic line has been truly different from the general outflow of mass-produced pop. Their latest release, 'The Visitors', is an extremely enjoyable album of traditional high quality in sound, production and execution – a delight to listen to in every respect. ABBA are head and shoulders above anything in a similar vein. The four members of ABBA are consummate professionals backed by top-notch personnel and it shows on every note sung and played on this album."

With the release of 'The Visitors', ABBA talked about the songs featured on the album and gave their own personal views on various songs:

The Visitors (Crackin- Up)
AGNETHA – "I like The Visitors very much because it is a bit original and different for us".

BJORN – "It is up to everyone to decide what the lyrics to "The Visitors" mean. I am not saying what the song is about because it is full of double meanings."

FRIDA – "Bjorn told me what this song meant after we had recorded it, but he wanted to keep it as a secret, so I'll respect that. In fact, it's a philosophical song. Anyone can have his own appreciation of it and then it won't be misunderstood. I spent more than 15 days preparing my voice to the right sound for this song."

Head Over Heels
AGNETHA – "It's a different lyric. I think it's a very happy song. I can see this crazy girl in front of me. It felt good to sing this song because I felt very cool and I think you can hear that – it is a different way to sing."

Soldiers
AGNETHA – "Well, I see the lyrics very seriously and I think every human being is a bit afraid of what can happen in the world. The situation doesn't feel too good. It's about the fear of what can happen."

BJORN – "Soldiers' is not about ordinary fighting men, but about those in high rank, those military men who make decisions that the politicians don't even know about."

Two For The Price Of One
BJORN – "Actually, there were only three or four players on this song, the rest is all 'synthies'."

Slipping Through My Fingers

AGNETHA – "I enjoyed making 'Slipping Through My Fingers' the most. It felt very 'true' to do because the situation is like that with our daugther when she goes to school. Although they are Bjorn's thoughts, they are mine too. I suppose, I think he has captured them very well."

Like An Angel Passing Through My Room

FRIDA – "This song is full of good memories for me. We were the only two, Benny and I in the studio, alone with the 'tic tock' sound. I love this sort of song.

AGNETHA – "I am not there at all. There is a watch in the background which is really a keyboard. I think it is a strange number because you wait for something that never comes. We did two or three different backing tracks for this number and none of them came out that good. So we tried a lot of different sounds and things and nothing worked. Then they tried this very 'naked' approach and I think it sounds a bit exciting, but I have a feeling that it doesn't happen, although I still like it. It is strong enough as a melody but I am not sure it has been given the right treatment."

Worldwide advance orders for 'The Visitors' were phenomenal; 700,000 copies in England, 600,000 copies in Germany, 500,000 copies in America and 300,000 copies in Sweden. During its first week of release, 'The Visitors' went straight to number one in England, Germany, Holland, Sweden, Belgium and Denmark.

As 'The Visitors' continued to make its mark throughout the world during December, Agnetha, Benny, Bjorn and Frida concentrated on matters away from ABBA. On 1st December, Benny married his girlfriend, Mona Noeklit, at a secret ceremony in Stockholm. Both Benny and Bjorn were now spending the majority of their time with their wives, as both were expecting babies over the forthcoming Christmas period. "I'm not reading any novels now, just books on babycare" said Benny, whilst Bjorn said "It's the best Christmas present anyone could wish for."

However, it was during December that Benny and Bjorn's 'dream' of writing a musical looked like becoming a reality when world-famous musical lyricist Tim Rice travelled to Stockholm to talk to Benny and Bjorn about a possible Andersson/Rice/Ulvaeus collaboration in the future. On a recent visit to America, it was New York theatre producer Richard Vos who first informed Tim Rice of Benny and Bjorn's great wish to write a musical. Tim therefore wasted no time, and visited Stockholm to find out more from the men themselves. After spending a few days talking, the Andersson/Rice/Ulvaeus partnership was forged.

Frida too was forging a new partnership with British singer/songwriter Phil Collins. Frida had decided that during 1982 she would record her first solo album in English and had asked Phil Collins to produce the album for her. Phil was more than happy to accept the offer and, together with Frida, spent much of December auditioning over five hundred songs for their forthcoming Lyngstad/Collins production.

Meanwhile, Agnetha was enjoying great solo success in Sweden together with her daughter, Linda. Their album Nu Tandas Tusen Julelijus, which they had recorded the previous year, was released with great success throughout Scandanavia. Before Christmas it had sold 70,000 copies, making it the biggest-selling Christmas album ever released in Sweden.

133

As the year came to an end Agnetha, Benny, Bjorn and Frida reflected upon another successful and highly productive year for ABBA. One thing was for sure, with the prospect of new ABBA records, together with solo projects, 1982 looked certain to be equally as successful and productive.

CHAPTER TWENTY ONE
THE FIRST TEN YEARS

1982 began with Agnetha, Benny, Bjorn and Frida all taking a break from ABBA in order to pursue personal and individual activities. During the first two weeks of January, both Benny and Bjorn once again became fathers. Bjorn and Lena were the first to celebrate the birth of their daughter, Emma, on Janaury 3rd, followed by Benny and Mona, who on January 10yth celebrated the birth of their son, Ludvig. Therefore, needless to say, for the first few months of 1982, Benny's and Bjorn's priorities lay firmly at home with their wives and children.

With this welcome break from ABBA activities, Agnetha also seized the opportunity to indulge herself with family life, whilst Frida took the first step to review her solo career. During February, Frida recorded her first solo album in English at Polar Studios, together with Phil Collins and a host of internationally-respected musicians. On January 5th ABBA's first single of the year was released throughout some European countries – 'Head Over Heels'/'The Visitors', whilst in America and Australia. 'When All Is Said And Done' was released. Despite both single releases making an immediate impact on the charts, neither managed to break into the Top Ten. The fact that both singles were included on the now multi-selling 'Visitors' album probably meant that those who would want the songs had them already.

During March, ABBA made the headlines around the world after it was reported that they had been banned by the Russian authorities. In America ABBA had allowed their video for 'When All Is Said And Done' to be included in an American television programme in which artists and celebrities protested against the Russian infiltration of Poland. When the programme 'Let Poland Be Poland' was screened on March 13th, it seemed that the Russian authorities were not too pleased with ABBA's involvement, via their video. The following day this report was relayed by a journalist working in Russia: "It has been playing to packed houses, but 'ABBA The Movie' was mysteriously replaced by another film at cinemas here today. No reason has been given for its removal but there is a strong rumour that it is due to ABBA's video of 'When All Is Said And Done' appearing on last night's 'Let Poland Be Poland' television programme."

When asked for a comment about the report, Benny said "We'll lose a lot of money by being banned in Russia, but all we are worried about is that our fans are being denied the chance to hear our music."

During April Benny and Bjorn began writing new material for ABBA, and also found the time to compose the theme tune for the 1982 World Ice Hockey Championships, due to be held in Gothenburg during the summer. In the meantime, the population of America once again witnessed a mass ABBA promotional campaign in the form of 'ABBA Weekend USA'. For the whole weekend during Easter holidays ABBA's records received priority airplay thoughout American radio stations. Backed my mass media advertising, 'ABBA Weekend USA' was a resounding success and concluded with an exclusive 90-minute interview with ABBA, conducted by American DJ Bob Hamilton, which was broadcast simultaneously by over three hundred radio stations.

May saw ABBA back at Polar Studios where they recorded a selection of new songs: 'Just Like That', 'I Am The City', 'The Day Before You Came', 'Under Attack', 'Cassandra' and 'You Owe Me One'. However, only two of these new songs were to be included on ABBA's next album release, which was to be a double album of all ABBA single releases to date. In total 23 songs would be featured on this compilation album, ranging from 1972 to 1982, and would be a unique collection aimed to celebrate ABBA's ten years as a recording entity.

During the summer Agnetha, Benny, Bjorn and Frida once again concentrated on projects away from ABBA. Benny and Bjorn were now working with ideas for their possible future musical collaboration with Tim Rice. Frida, whose solo album was scheduled for an August release, embarked on an intensive worldwide promotional tour, whilst Agnetha realised her acting ambition and made a Swedish film, 'Raskenstam', in which she protrayed a leading character. However, by early October, Agnetha, Benny, Bjorn and Frida were reunited as ABBA for promotional reasons in connection with their forthcoming album and single releases. On October 8th, ABBA broke their ten-month silence and released a new single titled 'The Day Before You Came'/'Cassandra'. Throughout Europe it quickly placed ABBA back in the Top Ten single charts. However, in England the story was different.

Despite making an immediate impact on the charts, 'The Day Before You Came' failed to reach a higher position that 32. Had the bubble burst or was everybody waiting to obtain the song on the forthcoming compilation album release? During the first week of November ABBA began arriving in England for the launch of their new album, 'ABBA The Singles (The First Ten Years)'.

Agnetha was the first to arrive in London, on November 3rd, and seized the opportunity to do some Christmas shopping before ABBA activities took over. Just before midnight that same day, Frida arrived direct from her solo promotional tour of America. When Benny and Bjorn arrived the following day, the ABBA jigsaw was complete and preparations could finally begin for the tenth anniversary celebrations and album launch. At 11am on Friday 5th November, ABBA opened the proceedings and held a mass photo session at their hotel for the world's press, which was followed by numerous newspaper, magazine and radio interviews. During their many interviews, ABBA reflected upon their ten years as a group and also discussed their future plans.

FRIDA – "Benny and Bjorn were recording an album of their own ('Lycka') and for one song they needed a female choir ('Hej Gamle Man') so it was very natural to ask Agnetha and myself if we wanted to do that part. We did, and thought it sounded very good. Then we decided to try something in English, so Benny and Bjorn wrote a song with English lyrics and the title of that song was 'People Need Love', and that's now we started, actually."

BJORN – "The first REAL manifestation of ABBA? Probably on a track called 'Hej Gamle Man'. We knew the girls and invited them to come into the studio to sing backing vocals. It sounded very good – it had a special sound and that's when we realised the potential of the girls' voices together."

"AMERICA:"
BENNY – "As the situation is in America, when things start moving there all the bands and artists move over the America and work from there, so they are available all the time for anybody who wants them in person. We talked about that a couple of years ago and I don't think any of us was really prepared to do that again, after having done exactly the same thing in Europe and other parts of the world to acheive the popularity that we have."

"FAVOURITE SONGS:"

AGNETHA – "My favourite is 'The Winner Takes It All'. I think it's a very good song – very good melody and very good lyrics. I think it's a whole song, it goes in a roll – it never stops in a way, it just goes together."

"WHAT HAS BEEN MORE INSTRUMENTAL IN THE SUCCESS OF ABBA, THE MUSIC OR THE GIRLS' APPEARANCES?"

BJORN – "Both, it's a combination. There's no way you can say afterwards tht this was more important than the other – but I'd like to think that the music comes first."

"WHAT DO YOU THINK OF EACH OTHER TEN YEARS ON?"

BJORN – "Do you really want to know?"

BENNY – "I think of them as friends from such a long way back."

FRIDA – "I think of them as people I can rely on one hundred per cent and, of course, as professional collaborators".

"DO YOU STILL GET ON WELL?"

AGNETHA – "Yes, very much so, Bjorn and I have personal contact every day because of the children and we get along very well. As for Benny and Frida, I don't see them that much of course, apart from when the group gets together, which is quite often anyway."

"THE FUTURE:"

BENNY – "I don't know if there is anything more to acheive, how could there be? Not by selling records. Not by going on the road. Not by writing even better songs for ABBA. I think it's sort of never started and never ended. I feel, personally, I'm very keen to start something else – something new, something more."

BJORN – "We have in fact had some discussions with Tim Rice in London about a possible collaboration. We don't know yet but we hope we'll be able to write a musical soon with him."

AGNETHA – "I think I'll have to stay in this business, I don't know anything else so much. I feel very comfortable in this business and I think I'll stay in it and work with what I'm doing or maybe I'll be a producer or maybe I'll get into the movie world."

BJORN – "I would say that what I would like to acheive with ABBA is to make an even better album that would be by our standards – and by the audience's standards – the best one.

By early afternoon all interviews and photo sessions had been successfully completed and ABBA made their way to The Belfry Club in London's Belgravia, where an exclusive and lavish celebration party was held in their honour. The highlight of the party came when CBS Chairman, Maurice Oberstein, presented ABBA with a presentation frame containing all 23 of their single releases pressed in nine carat gold.

The following day it was time for ABBA to face the television cameras at the BBC Television Centre. In the morning Agnetha and Benny made a special appearance on the live children's programme 'Saturday Superstore', and in the evening the complete ABBA were special guests on Noel Edmond's 'Late Late Breakfast Show'.

ABBA

ABBA

After spending the whole day at the television studios, at 10pm Agnetha, Benny, Bjorn and Frida decided to relax at La Nassa restrurant in Chelsea, together with a few close friends. Among the people joining ABBA was Tim Rice, who had just officially decided to work with Benny and Bjorn on a musical project beginning in 1983. On Sunday November 7th, ABBA travelled to Germany where a further three days of promotion and celebrations lay ahead of them. Once again, ABBA conducted several press interviews and photo sessions, and also attended another celebration party arranged by Polydor Records. The appeared on the television programme 'Show Express' where they sang three of their more recent songs, 'The Day Before You Came', 'Cassandra' and 'Under Attack', before the live and very enthusiastic studio audience.

On November 10th, ABBA released their anniversary album 'ABBA The Singles (The First Ten Years)', featuring 23 songs: 'Ring Ring', 'Waterloo', 'So Long', 'I Do I Do I Do I Do I Do', 'SOS', 'Mamma Mia', 'Fernando', 'Dancing Queen', 'Money Money Money', 'Knowing Me Knowing You', 'The Name Of The Game', 'Take A Chance On Me', 'Summer Night City', 'Chiquitita', 'Does Your Mother Know', 'Voulez Vous', 'Gimmie Gimmie Gimmie (A Man After Midnight)', 'I Have A Dream', 'The Winner Takes It All', 'Super Trouper', 'One Of Us', 'The Day Before You Came' and 'Under Attack'.

Predictably, 'The Singles' became an immediate worldwide success and placed ABBA at the top of the album charts around the world. Critically, The Singles was probably best summed up in this review by Christopher Connelly from America's Rolling Stone magazine, who awarded the album a maximum five stars: "This twenty-three song collection confirms what a lucky few in the US have known for some time: ABBA is the greatest pop band of the last ten years. There are more infectious melodies, grabby hooks and danceable drum beats on one side of this two-disc set than in most artists' entire catalogues. Even a casual listen to side one's first five songs – 'Ring Ring', 'Waterloo', 'So Long', 'I Do I Do I Do I Do I Do' and 'SOS' – should make for one of the peppiest sessions you're likely to have in a long time. Benny Andersson and Bjorn Ulvaeus' production is so pristine and the always perfect singing of Frida and Agnetha, either solo or blending together, is as refreshing as a blast of Scandanavia air. 'The Singles' provides an ideal introduction to this talented and highly influential band. Buy this, okay?"

As December arrived ABBA were back at home in Stockholm, where they continued with various promotional activities. On December 3rd 'Under Attack'/'You Owe Me One' was released as a single and quickly placed ABBA in the Top Ten throughout Europe. However, in England, probably due to its inclusion on the current number one album, 'The Singles', 'Under Attack' failed to reach the Top Twenty and peaked at 26. Once again, it seemed that everybody who would want the song had it already, on album.

During December ABBA made two 'live' appearances on television, one in England and one in Sweden. On December 11th ABBA appeared 'live via satellite' from Stockholm on Noel Edmonds' 'Late Late Breakfast Show', where they sang 'Under Attack' and 'I Have A Dream'. The following week ABBA appeared on Swedish television and gave a 'live' rendition of 'Thank-You For The Music'. This was to be ABBA's final television appearance for four years. As December ended it became clear that Agnetha, Benny, Bjorn and Frida were all planning to concentrate on solo projects away from ABBA in the future. During their ten years together ABBA had reached the pinnacle of their profession and achieved heights in popular music that were unparalleled by any other group. There was nothing left for ABBA to achieve, at least for the time being, and so it was with much enthusiasm that Agnetha, Benny, Bjorn and Frida decided it was time to move on . . .

CHAPTER TWENTY TWO
FRIDA – 'GOING ON'

In more ways than one February 1981 marked a major change in the life of Anni-Frid Lyngstad. On a personal level, it was now that Frida suddenly found herself alone when her twelve-year relationship with Benny had ended in divorce. Professionally, although unbeknown to Frida at the time, it was during this period that she was introduced to a fellow artist and musician who, in twelve months' time, would take her career to new heights.

In an attempt to escape the mass-media attention surrounding her divorce announcement Frida, together with her daughter Lotta, retreated to their summer house miles from Stockholm in search of peace and tranquility. Whilst driving to their house, Lotta was playing a cassette of mixed songs on the car stereo when suddenly one particular song grabbed her mother's attention. The song? – 'In The Air Tonight'. The artist? – Phil Collins. "I liked it so much" recalled Frida, "I felt that this was a really strong song." Inspired to hear more of Phil Collins work, Frida quickly bought herself a copy of his latest album, 'Face Value', and immediately 'fell in love with it.'

It was during the autumn of 1981, after completing her seventh album with ABBA, that Frida felt that the time was right to renew her solo career, and so decided to record her first solo album in English. However, there was one condition – Phil Collins would have to be her producer. "I liked 'Face Value' so much I must have listened to it almost every day for eight months" recalled Frida. "In particular Phil's arrangements and drum sound impressed me, so when it came up that I was going to do a solo album, my first and only thought was to have Phil as my producer. Without him I wouldn't have gone ahead – I wanted him that much"." To Frida's great delight Phil readily agreed to produce her album and a new and potentially exciting musical partnership was formed.

Almost immediately Frida, together with Phil, began auditioning songs for their project. "I got from different record companies about five hundred songs, and none of the songs were suitable I thought, so we had to go out to ask different companies if they were interested to write for me, or if they had something I could use" said Frida. "The songs that were finally picked I had one hundred percent feeling for, and they were chosen from my heart."

'SOMETHIN'S GOIN' ON'

1)	'Tell Me It's Over'	*(Stephen Bishop)*
2)	'I See Red'	*(Jim Rafferty)*
3)	'I Got Something'	*(Tomas Ledin)*
4)	'Strangers'	*(Jayni Bradbury/Dave Morris)*
5)	'To Turn To Stone'	*(Peter Belotle/Giorgio Moroder)*
6)	'I Know There's Something Going On'	*(Russ Ballard)*
7)	'Threnody'	*(Dorothy Parker/Per Gessle)*
8)	'Baby Don't You Cry No More'	*(Rod Argent)*
9)	'The Way You Do'	*(Bryan Ferry)*
10)	'You Know What I Mean'	*(Phil Collins)*
11)	'Here We'll Stay' (duet with Phil Collins)	*(Tony Colton/Jean Roussel)*

On February 15th 1982, Frida began recording her solo album at Polar Music Studios, Stockholm, together with Phil and his team of musicians: Keyboards: Peter Robinson, Guitars: Daryl Stuermer, Bass: Mo Foster, Drums, percussion and backing vocals: Phil Collins, Phenix Hornes, Saxophones: Don Myrick, Trumpets: Michael Harris, Rahmlee M Davis, Trombone: Louis Satterfield, (courtesy of Earth Wind & Fire). Strings: The Martyn Ford Orchestra, Harp: Skailla Knnga, Engineer: Hugh Padgham, Assistant Engineer: 'Paris' Edvinsson. After spending six weeks at Polar Studios, Frida's first solo album for seven years, was complete. At the press launch of the album, held at Polar Studios, Frida and Phil began to talk about their first musical collaboration.

Frida – "ABBA has been working for ten years now and in a way I felt that I was stuck in a pattern. As my life has changed so completely in other respects, I feel that it is a necessity to change even the musical aspect of my life because I feel so strongly for it."

Phil – "When I first started to work with Frida I was a bit in awe. I mean, whether you like ABBA or not, I like some of their earlier stuff, although I was never an ABBA fan. But you know, when Frida was standing there, she has an aura because you know how incredibly powerful that band was."

Frida – "I remember, the first week I was pretty nervous because it was the first thing I'd ever done outside ABBA, and all the people were new for me. I had met Phil twice and the others I had not met at all, so I was very, very tense and nervous. I soon felt that they were a group of very nice people so after a week we really had it together. It was a very relaxed situation and very nice atmosphere. I really loved to work together with Phil's musicians. They have been so friendly and so nice to me – all of them."

Phil – "The first two or three weeks in the studio, no-one stopped laughing and that was very important – it loosened everybody up. It was easy to say something was crap because there was a lot of laughing going on. If something was crap there was no bad vibes like you can't say anything."

Frida – "I think it meant a lot that Phil had gone through a divorce, as I did a year ago, and out of that he wrote a lot of songs on 'Face Value'. I felt very strongly for his lyrics, I mean, it had a big deal to do with how I used to feel. I felt that we had something in common, both musically and experience-wise."

Phil – "I think Frida was the injured party in the same way I was in my divorce. Frida mentioned yesterday that for about eight months she was basically not just listening to my record, but really listening to it, and I guess that it twanged a few strings with her."

Frida – "It wasn't the same as making an ABBA record. With those, Bjorn and Benny make the tapes and Agnetha and I put the vocals on afterwards. This time I was in the studio with the band day and night for six weeks, rehearsing each song together before any recording was done. In many ways it was easier than working on ABBA material. This was MY project and I knew what I wanted – there was no need for any compromise. I can honestly say I have no doubts about the end results."

Phil – "At first Frida was very insecure because she's always been told what to do in ABBA by Benny and Bjorn. I would go in there and stir up a hornet's nest because Stig Andersson wanted one of Benny and Bjorn's songs on the album – a song that hadn't even been written – because he wanted to keep it in the family."

"I said, "Well, listen, this song is not yet written and it's not going to go on the album unless we like it – it's not a foregone conclusion.' And Frida was saying, "Quite right. Quite right." I think with this first album Frida has gained a lot of strength, being able actually not to be told what to do. I just said to her, "You do it. It's your album. You sing the way you want to . . .""

Frida – "This album is very much Frida. I love this album. It is *MY* album. Through it I hope people can get to know me a little more than they would by listening to an ABBA album."

During August 1982, 'Somethings Going On' was released worldwide together with the title song, 'I Know There's Something Going On', as a single. With the release of both the album and the single, Frida embarked on an intensive promotional tour which took her to England, Germany, France, Austria, Holland, Denmark, Finland, Sweden, Switzerland, America and Canada. In each country she met the press and appeared on numerous television and radio shows.

"*'Something's Going On'*
offers intelligently
and skillfully
crafted pop."

Critcially, Frida received much praise for her debut international solo album, which seemed to be best summed up in this review by Christopher Hill, for Record Magazine: "Phil Collins, British art-rocker with a taste for funk, is perhaps the ideal producer to give ABBA-component Anni-Frid Lyngstad a fully-fleshed musical persona. The woman that emerges on 'Something's Going On' is a versatile and highly polished entertainer. As a singer Frida is shown to be more interesting than in her ABBA work. The electric material from Bryan Ferry to Russ Ballard is finely calculated to stretch her talent without revealing its breaking point. 'Something's Going On' offers intelligently and skillfully crafted pop."

Commercially, 'Something's Going On' was also very well received and worldwide sales exceeded two million copies. In France, Germany, Holland, Denmark, Finland, Norway and Canada 'Something Going On' was certified 'gold' whilst in Sweden it achieved 'platinum' status. The single, 'I Know There's Something Going On', also provided Frida with a top twenty hit throughout Europe but, perhaps surprisingly, enjoyed it's biggest success in America, where it peaked at number thirteen on the Billboard charts.

In late 1982 Frida was asked by a Swedish journalist "What reaction have you received for 'Something's Going On'?, to which Frida happily replied, "The welcome has been fantastic, so positive everywhere. Everything is just great now."

1983 began with Frida drastically changing her home environment after she made the decision to leave Sweden and make a new life for herself in England. It seemed that years of being following everywhere by the Swedish press in Stockholm had finally forced Frida to find some privacy in another country, and so a luxurious flat in London's Mayfair became her new home. "I can walk on the streets in London as a normal person" said Frida. "The people there are not surprised when there is a famous person passing by, so in London I can live a quiet and anonymous life. In Stockholm I was always followed by journalists and I had the feeling that I was being suffocated. They have always been hard upon my heels. When I sat in a restaurant cosily, it was in the newspapers the following day. I could not suffer it any more."

From her new base, during 1983, Frida concentrated on only a few projects which left her with much more time to rest and take life more easily. Firstly, in early February Frida attended the San Remo Song Festival in Italy, and whilst there also made an appearance on the Italian programme 'Pop Call'.

During March she went to France in order to make a special appearance in a screen version of 'ABBACADABRA', a fairytale musical adventure story set to music of ABBA. In the screen version Frida played the part of a Princess called La Belle and all filming was carried out at the Castle of Usse, Western France. A cast album of 'ABBACADABRA' was also recorded, where Frida sang a duet titled 'Belle' together with her co-star, Daniel Balavoine. When released as a single in France, 'Belle' became a sizeable hit, and Frida and Daniel sang their duet on a few television programmes throughout France. During July, Frida found herself filming once again after accepting a small role in her second Swedish movie, titled 'Jokerfys'. In the film she portrays a character called Louise, the secretary and mistress of a factory owner whose family is trying to kill. 'Jokerfys', a comedy/thriller, starred Swedish actor/comedian Magnus Harenstam, and all filming took palce in Ekero, a suburb of Stockholm, Sweden. Of her latest film role, Frida said "I find this part much better, it has more character."

In September Frida recorded a duet with Scottish singer B.A. Robertson, titled 'Time', which was from the London production of 'ABBACADABRA'. When released as a single during December, 'Time' peaked at number forty-five on England's charts. As well as attending the premiere of 'ABBACADABRA' at the Lyric Theatre, London on December 8th, Frida also performed 'Time', together with B.A. Robertson, on two television programmes – The Russell Hartry Show and Nationwide.

After the premiere of 'ABBACADABRA', Frida was interviewed by a journalist and revealed that she was to record her second English-language solo album in early 1984. She also talked about ABBA and her long-term plans:

"Will there be another ABBA album?"
"Wait and see. There will be one more album at least, if only for the fans.."

"The fans:"
"Yes, it's the fans that made us, not ourselves. They bought the singles and the albums. If nobody had, we would not be where we are today. We owe them one more album."

"When ABBA decide officially to break up, what will you do?"
"Definitely settle down. I'll be nearly forty by then and that's too old to remain in the top pop business. When ABBA go, so shall I. I can't go on forever. I'll probably cast myself away on a desert island."

"You mean you will give up singing?"
"No, I could't do that – music is in my blood. No, I meant stopping being a superstar. I could always go back to the beginning and start over again, you know – talent contests and local shows. I must confess that I have selfish reasons, though. Being rich and famous isn't all happiness and at times the pressures have got to me."

"But people like Frank Sinatra and Dean Martin have gone into their seventies entertaining and making money."

"Money isn't everything – I'd still want to entertain, though. But constant jet-setting – absolutely never again."

'SHINE'

1)	'Shine'	*(Kevin Jarvis/Guy Fletcher/Jeremy Bird)*
2)	'One Little Lie'	*(Simon Climie/Kirsty McColl)*
3)	'The Face'	*(Daniel Balavoine/Kirsty McColl)*
4)	'Twist in the Dark'	*(Andee Leek)*
5)	'Slowly'	*(Benny Andersson/Bjorn Ulvaeus)*
6)	'Heart of the Country'	*(Stuart Adamson)*
7)	'Come To Me (I am Woman)'	*(Eddie Howell/David Dundas)*
8)	'Chemistry Tonight'	*(Peter Glenister/Simon Climie/Kirsty McColl)*
9)	'Don't Do It'	*(Anni-Frid Lyngstad)*
10)	'Comfort Me'	*(Peter Glenister)*

Exactly two years from recording 'Something's Going On', on February 15th, 1984, Friday began recording her second English-language solo album at Studios de la Grande Armee, Paris, France.

For her latest project Frida had chosen a producer as 'in vogue' as Phil Collins had been in 1982 – Steve Lillywhite who, at the age of twenty-nine, had already produced such established artists and bands as Simple Minds, U2, Joan Armatrading, Peter Gabriel, Big Country, Bruce Foxton, Siouxsie & The Banshees and Ultravox.

Together Frida and Steve assembled a team of respected and talented musicians to work with them on their musical collaboration, namely: Tony Levin (Bass), Rutger Gunnarsson (Bass), Peter Glenister (Electric & Acoustic Guitar), Simon Climie (Keyboards), Mark Brzezecki (Drums), Marc Chantreau (Percussion), Kirsty McColl (Backing Vocals), Simon Climie (Backing Vocals), Howard Gray & Frederic Defaye (Engineer & Assistant Engineer).

Taking six weeks to record, by April, Frida's latest album was complete and one again Frida concentrated on promotional business in connection with the album's latest release. During August and September, 'Shine' was released throughout Europe, together with the title track, 'Shine' as a single. At the press launch of the album, 'Shine' was described as ". . . a modern and unusual album and different from a purely musical point of view from the earlier releases. 'Shine' is tough, straightforward and openly sensitive. This is a very personal record with sharp contours and its own special sound, making it necessary to concentrate but at the same time giving so much more. 'Shine' is also the result of positive vibrations between Frida and her producer Steve Lillywhite. They themselves say that it is a combination of two souls with the same thought."

However, within weeks of its release, it soon became evident that both 'Shine' the album and 'Shine' the single were not going to be the success that Frida had hoped for. Despite embarking on an intensive promotional tour of Europe, during which she talked to the press and made several appearances on television in Germany, France, Holland, Denmark, Finland, Norway and Sweden, sales for 'Shine' were very disappointing and chart positions very low. Despite every effort to make 'Shine' a success, many people felt that Frida received very little support from her record companies. Perhaps if they had put as much effort into promoting 'Shine' as Frida had, both the album and the single releases would have gained the recognition they deserved. During November, Guy Bodescot, a founder of ABBA's French Fan Club, conducted an interview with Frida in which she spoke frankly about 'Shine' and, naturally, ABBA:

Guy – "Can you tell us about the promotion you have done to launch your new album, 'Shine'?"

Frida – "The same as last time, except I chose the best TV shows in the countries I had been invited. In all cases the audience ratings in these shown were very high. Apart from that, I met the press and radio and concentrated my effort on video promotion. I went in turn to Belgium, Holland, Germany, Scandanavia and France."

Guy – "What do you thing about the frequency of your visits to certain countries like Germany and Holland, and the total abscence of promotion in other countries like England, Italy and Spain?"

Frida – "I based my choice on the sales of my preceeding album. I went where it had sold most copies. For England it was different because I had received lots of invitations from TV shows, but when they learned that 'Heart Of The Country' had been chosen as a single by the record company, they cancelled all their invitations."

Guy – "Rumous are circulating that you wish to record a special album for the U.S.A., where you wish to launch yourself . . ."

Frida – "That's not true. We wanted to make another single apart from 'Shine' which would have been more suited to the U.S. market. But my album still hasn't come out in the U.S.A. and I don't know if it ever will. I no longer have any desire to make an effort for 'Shine'. I brought out an album and it didn't please the public – there's nothing I can do about it."

Guy – "How did your choide of Steve Lillywhite come about?"

Frida – "It was Thomas Johansson, my manager, who showed me what Steve had produced, especially Simple Minds, and I found it very good. I immediately accepted that we should meet. Steve was in touch with American publishers and composers who weren't very well known but who were very talented, and we all worked together. That was in fact what I enjoyed most. We created a family atmosphere, increasing our possibilities of co-operation. The critics reproached us for this, finding that it cut down originality, but that was not my opinion."

Guy – "This family atmosphere – you were already familiar with it from ABBA . . ."

Frida – "Yes, that's perhaps why I wanted to find it again. But I should like to insist once again on the fantastic nature of my collaboration with Phil Collins. At that time I didn't have any deep contact with musicians but I have now moved in this direction."

Guy – "A dream album for Frida would be one produced by Phil Collins but in the nice friendly atmosphere of Steve Lillywhite?"

Frida – "Yes, that would probably be a good idea".

Guy – "Have you seen Steve since the recording sessions?"

Frida- "No, but we are going to meet in December to discuss the impact of 'Shine' and its sales. We'll then consider another collaboration. If we get together again, the album will have to more commercial because I can't allow myself to record a disc that doesn't sell. I'd rather not bring out an album at all. I don't think there is much point in recording records which you can't sell. I'm still convinced that 'Shine' is an escellent album but it lacked a big hit, like 'Something's Going On', which would stand out from the general production. We thought that we had that with the title song – 'Shine' – but that song in my opinion is ahead of its time, it's too modern to be accepted by the general public. That doesn't mean that I regret my collaboration with Steve, because he carried out his work as producer to perfection, leaving my personal creativity to express itself freely."

Guy – "The producer must not impose his way of seeing things, is that right?"

Friday – "Yes, and that's what Steve respected. The artist must feel at ease with his producer, and must be able to rely on him. The perfect relationship is not a mutual attraction but rather an emotional and musical vibration. I must be able to let myself go at the microphone without fear and without feeling any stress. This is the moment when the producer must intervene and help me to express my musical sensibility."

Guy – "At our last meeting in the Paris studioes, you talked about Sting as a producer."

Frida – "Yes, I had been in contact with him and he was very interested in my project. I admire Sting for her personality and also becase 'The Police' are an excellent group. Unfortunately, our timetables didn't fit in with each other this time. But I was a little afraid that his very strong personality would have weighed a bit too heavily."

Guy – "When you wanted to launch yourself as a solo artiste, you had to bear the weight of ABBA. That has expressed itself, amongst other ways, by the support or rejection of the group's fans. How do you feel about your relationship with ABBA's public?"

Frida – "One thing is for certain, when I record I'm not concerned whether or not I give pleasure to ABBA's fans. If they like what I do and what I am, that's an honour for me, and that's the same for the other three members of ABBA as far as their solo careers are concerned. I want just as much to please another audience, an audience which never listens to ABBA, and I've already managed that, especially here in France. On the other hand, I will never turn my back on what I lived through with ABBA. If I am what I am, I owe it to ABBA. ABBA has brough me everything as far as my maturity and professionalism are concered. It's not that I am trying to do something different from ABBA, that I reject that period with the group. I am proud to be a member of ABBA, because ABBA was, a few years ago, the biggest group in the world, both as far as sales and popularity go. I shall never be as important as ABBA, because that is impossible. ABBA was at the top – as far as you can go."

Guy – "At the time of your last TV show, which you did with Benny and Bjorn in Paris, April 1984, Michel Drucker asked Bjorn if ABBA would ever sing again, and Bjorn replied 'Ask the girls'. Our impression was that each member of ABBA was blaming the others for the lack of activity of the group. What do you think?"

Frida – "I understand your impression, and I think the problem is not to know who is responsible for this lack of activity, but rather to determine what ABBA could do as a group. There is no question for us to go back into the studio to make a record like the ones which we made before. If we work together again as a group, we shall have to bring something new. For my part I think that I shall come back to ABBA, but when that happens it won't be enough for me to say "I want to sing with ABBA", I'll need to propose an original concept to the three other members, and they'll have to accept that project."

Guy – "That won't be easy because since 1981 you've evolved in totally different directions. Do you think that Agnetha and yourself would accept playing the same role as simply singers in ABBA?"

Frida – "Certainly not, but I'm just as sure that Bjorn and Benny would't want to work like before, and that they would envisage a different form of collaboration. We'll never go back to the original situation. If there is to be a new ABBA, it will have evolved from the old one."

Since 1985, Frida has lived a relatively anonymous life in Majorca, Switzerland and Sweden. "I have no plans – I live from day to day. I do not know if I will release any more records – I have been treated very badly by the record companies. Now I can do what I want, that I never earlier had the chance to do", said Frida.

In January 1987 Frida made the headlines in Sweden after recording a duet with the Sweden group 'Ratata'. The song titled 'As Long As I Have You', was recorded amid great secrecy in Stockholm during December 1986. Frida also appeared on the promotional video to accompany the song. The Swedish press reported that Frida was making a comeback to the music business; however, Frida's manager, Gorel Hanser, was quick to deny these rumours and said "Frida's participation on the record was just a casual stop back to the music business and was not yet a question of a comeback". Nevertheless, when released as a single throughout Scandanavia in January 1987, 'As Long As I Have You' was an immediate Top 5 hit.

The beginning of the 90's has seen Frida actively involved with environmental issues, and she is currently involved with two environmentalist groups – 'Der Naturaliga Steget' (The Natual Step) and 'Artister For Jiluo' (Artists for the World).

In December 1990 Frida made a rare and unexpected appearance on Swedish TV, where she talked about her new work with environmental issues. Frida also organised a large benefit concert which was staged in Stockholm on Wednesday 14th August 1991. Frida had gathered together a host of top Swedish artists and musicians who all donated their time and performed, free of charge, to help raise funds for the 'Artists of the World' organisation. As well as organising the concert, Frida was also due to host the show; however, on the day, she failed to make an appearance. The rumour circulating was that Frida was 'too nervous' to face a live audience again and so had returned to her home in Switzerland.

151

However, the following year, on 28th January 1982, Frida did make a return to the stage, when she joined Swedish band, Roxette, live on stage at their concert in Zurich, Switzerland. Together, Frida and Roxette performed the classic ABBA song, 'Money Money Money'. Frida was also on stage again on 14th August 1992, at a second 'Artists For Miljo' benefit concert in Stockholm, which she has also organised. During the concert, which featured a host of top Swedish musicians, including Roxette, Frida performed her first single release for five years – 'Anglamark', together with a cover version of the Julian Lennon song, 'Saltwater'. Released to raise awareness and money for the 'Artist's For Miljo' organisation, the single became an immediate hit throughout Scandanavia.

Amid great secrecy, on 28th August 1992, Frida married her longtime boyfriend, Prince Ruzzo Ruess von Plauen – a German architect. The wedding ceremony took place in Denmark, after which, Frida and her husband returned to their home in Fribourg, Switzerland. Today, Frida is continuing to be a strong campaigner for her environmental groups.

CHAPTER TWENTY THREE
CHESS

After spending more than ten years writing, recording and performing their songs with ABBA, in January 1983 Benny and Bjorn expanded their songwriting capabilities, changed direction and began composing the music for their first musical collaboration together with lyricist Tim Rice. When Tim first went to meet Benny and Bjorn in Stockholm during December 1981, he presented them with several ideas of subjects on which they could base their musical. From the list of ideas, it was the story of an East versus West World Championship chess match that most appealed to Benny and Bjorn.

'We were very excited about 'Chess' from the beginning', said Bjorn. "The idea originated back in 1981 when Andrew Lloyd-Webber was busy with 'Cats' and Tim Rice was looking for other writers to collaborate with. Benny and I were mentioned, but Tim didn't think we would be able to fit it in. What he didn't know was that Benny and I had been dreaming about something like this for years. Tim had the original storyline for 'Chess' before he even approached us, and we thought the idea fascinating. It had interesting characters and the underlying suspense of the East versus West conflict. The principle figures are a Russian chess-master and his America opponent – though the musical is more about people and relationships that the game itself. The Russian falls for the American's wife and it develops from there".

In February 1983, Benny, Bjorn and Tim spent four days in the Russian capital, Moscow, in order to sample a little of the Russian way of life. "Part of the musical's action takes place in Moscow so we decided to spend a few days there to find out a little about what kind of people the Russians are" said Benny. "The visit has given us many positive impressions that we have to sort out when we get back to Stockholm."

For the remainder of 1983, Benny and Bjorn worked solidly, composing the music to 'Chess' – putting their music on to tapes and sending them to Tim so that he could add the lyrics. "We worked from 10am to 5pm, five days a week, for a year – me playing the piano, Bjorn playing guitar, and together playing around with different tunes" said Benny.

'CHESS'
Act One:
'Merano'
'Where I Want To Be' – The Russian and Molokov
'Opening Ceremony'
'Quartet' (A model of decorum and tranquility)
'Nobody's Side' – The American and Florence
'Chess'
'Mountain Duet'
'Florence Quits'
'Embassy Lament'
'Anthem'

Act Two:
'Bangkok'/'One Night In Bangkok'
'Heaven Help My Heart'
'Argument'
'I Know Him So Well'
'The Deal '(No Deal)
'Pity The Child'
'Endgame'
Epilogue:- 'You and I'/'The Story of Chess'

In January 1984 Benny, Bjorn and Tim began recording 'Chess' at Polar Music Studios, Stockholm, together with a host of well-known and respected British and Swedish artists and musicians.

CHESS
The principle singers:
Elaine Paige (Florence)
Murray Head (The American)
Tommy Korberg (The Russian)
Denis Quilly (Molokov)
Barbara Dickson (Svetlana)
Bjorn Skiffs (The Arbiter)

Choir:
The Ambrosian Singers

Backing Vocals:
Anders Glenmark, Karin Glenmark, Liza Ohman.

The Musicians:
Per Lindvall – Drums and Percussion
Lasse Wellander – Guitars
Rutger Gunnarsson – Bass
Benny Andersson/Anders Eljas – Synthesizers and Keyboards
Bjorn Jason Lindh – Flute
The London Symphony Orchestra
Engineered and mixed by Michael B. Tretor
Produced by Benny, Bjorn and Tim

On Friday October 26th, the double album recording of 'Chess' was released worldwide together with the accompanying single release, 'One Night In Bangkok', by Murray Head. In order to launch 'Chess' throughout Europe on Saturday 27th October, the artists and musicians featured on the album, together with Benny, Bjorn and Tim, embarked on a remarkable sell-out 'Chess in Concert' tour of Europe, where they performed five concerts in five days. Beginning at London's Barbican Centre, the tour proceeded to La Salle Playtel, Paris, Concertgebouw, Amsterdam, CCH, Hamburg and ended at the Berwaldhallen, Stockholm. "The tour went very well" said Bjorn. "We had to move about 225 people, I think every night from city to city, which was very difficult – but we managed."

When asked "Why go to all that trouble and expense to launch the album?", Bjorn replied, "I ask myself that question sometimes. But the truth is that we though it was the best promotionl we could do for one thing – and the other being that when 'Chess' comes into the theatre, it will be impossible to have that many people. I mean, you can't have more than thirty musicians in the theatre. So we wanted to hear what it all sounded like under the ultimate circumstances. It did cost a fortune but fortunately we had a sponsor." The 'Chess In Concert' tour was a resounding success and provided the new Andersson/ Rice/Ulvaeus muscial with an enormous amount of publicity.

Both the album and the single release were an immediate hit throughout Europe. The album achieved Top Ten positions throughout the European charts while the single, 'One Night In Bangkok', sold in excess of four million copies worldwide after reaching number one in Australia, Austria, Israel, Germany, South Africa, Sweden, Denmark, France, Holland, Belgium, Norway and Switzerland. In America, two different versions on 'One Night In Bangkok' both achieved Top Ten positions. With the successful release of 'Chess', Benny, Bjorn and Tim began talking about their first musical collaboration:

BENNY – "For a long time Bjorn and I have been talking about how great it would be if there was a chance for us to move into the music theatre. So when Tim came to us in Stockholm and asked if we wanted to collaborate with him – we seized the chance."

TIM – "It's not much about chess – as chess players. It's a story of the people who are in the chess world and you don't have to know a thing about chess to understand the play. It's really about a Russian chess player who becomes World Champion, and, at the moment of his victory, defects to the West. And it's about his problems when he gets to the West – his romantic problems – his political problems – his chess playing problems and his readjusting to a new life. In the end, one wonders perhaps if he is going to return to Russia because of his problems. It's wonderfully complicated like all the best operas."

BJORN – "Writing for the theatre is of course different from writing pop music. The actual process isn't – you sit down, write and work – that's the same. But there is a difference, first of all in where the ideas come from. In the theatre you are given the scenes and a sense of what is happening dramatically is provided. With a pop song, you just play around with rhythms and chords, and suddenly something will come up that is worth pursuing."

TIM- "This is the first time Benny and Bjorn have actually tried to write a piece of music that lasts for ninety minutes. It's quite a change from writing great pop songs that last four or five minutes to writing two albums' worth of continuous music – and I think that it is quite remarkable what they've done".

BENNY- "For Bjorn and myself, we wanted to have a grip on the whole project. We are very familiar with the recording studio – we felt at home recording because we have been doing it for so long. Therefore we wanted to hear it all first, on record, before it ended up on stage. If you record it first, you know that this is the best way that it can sound."

TIM- "Benny and Bjorn have this exquisite skill in the recording studio. They are masters of recorded sound. for two years our number one concern was to make a great record. It will be the director's job to make it a great show.

In January 1985, a second single from 'Chess' was released: "I Know Him So Well' by Elaine Paige and Barbara Dickson. Within weeks, 'Chess' had achieved a second worldwide smash hit single release as it topped the charts almost everywhere it was released. In England alone, 'I Know Him So Well' remained at number one for four weeks after selling over one million copies.

During 1985 and early 1986 preparations began to bring 'Chess' to the stage. American director Michael Bennett was put in charge of the production but, due to ill-health, was later replaced by British director Trevor Nunn. The cast of fifty-one was headed by Elaine Paige, Murray Head and Tommy Korbert.

On Wednesday 14th May 1986, amid a blaze of publicity, 'Chess' opened in London's West End at the Prince Edward Theatre. Amongst the 1,650 people attending the premiere were many famous people including Frida and , naturally, Benny and Mona, Bjorn and Lena and Tim. Costing four million pounds to stage, 'Chess' was in imediate hit with the audience and critics alike.

"A Grand Master Of A Show" – Newsweek

"A Blockbusting Spectacle" – The Times

"Spectacular, Sensational, Absolutely Marvellous" – BBC TV

"CHESS is beautifully written and superbly structured entertainment that is warm, emotional, intelligent and consistently enthralling" – BBC Radio

"A bouyant, electric and stirring theatre score by Bjorn Ulvaeus and Benny Andersson" – The Observer.

"One of the most important home-grown scores and shows of the 80's" – International Tribune.

"Tim Rice is the wittiest lyricist we've had since Coward" – Punch

Two years from opening in London, on 28th April 1988 'Chess' opened on Broadway at The Imperial Theatre, New York City. Starring Judy Kuhn, David Carroll and Philip Casnoff, the Broadway production of 'Chess' differed from the original production in two ways. Firstly, the storyline was altered although the characters remained the same, and secondly Benny and Bjorn had written two songs specifically for this new production – 'Someone Else's Story' and 'Lullaby'. Public interest in 'Chess' was huge, with advance ticket bookings totalling two million pounds. However, this great interest in the show did not deter New York critics from directing some of their most scathing views at the show.

"CHESS is beautifully written and superbly structured entertainment that is warm, emotional, intelligent and consistently enthralling"

"It is a grim, ham-fisted endevour that puts a serious dent in the popular belief that London is the crucible for all that is worthwhile in the musical theatre" – Washington Post.

"This match is stalemate" – USA Today

"Depressing, Chess Bored" – New York Daily News – "Time Rice's new musical makes too many wrong moves to be a winner."

During April and May Benny and Bjorn spent much time in New York, where they were actively involved with rehearsals for 'Chess'. They also produced the Original Broadway Cast Album of 'Chess', which was recorded at The Record Plant, New York, on April 17th, May 15, 16th and 17th. However, in view of the critic's views of 'Chess', the general public soon lost interest in the production, and within six months 'Chess' was forced to close.

"It's incredible," said Bjorn. "We thought it would be the same as it was in Europe – people making up their minds themselves. For instance, in London you have twenty-five different newspapers, with twenty-five different opinions, and people come to see the show because they are interested in the name of whatever. But in America, people only listen to the critics. I would say that eighty per cent of the audience is not really intersted in what they're seeing. They're interested in going to Broadway, having a night out and seeing a 'hit' musical. It was fun while we were rehearsing and doing the album, but afterwards I was so disappointed. But next time we won't make the same mistakes. I'm sure if we'd done it the right way, it would still be running, no problem."

After nearly four highly successful years in London's West end, in 1990 'Chess' closed at the Prince Edward Theatre and began its first U.K. tour. Starring Rebecca Storn, Chris Corcoron and Maurice Clarke, the 'Chess' U.K. Tour opened at the Theatre Royal, Plymouth on Monday 19th March 1990 and continued for the following twelve months playing to sell-out audiences at numerous theatres in England, Ireland, Scotland and Wales. Similar tours of 'Chess' have also taken place throughout Europe with great success. Arrangements are also currently being made to stage 'Chess' in Australia. Almost ten years since its creation, 'Chess' is still being seen and enjoyed by thousands of people thoughout the world.

CHAPTER TWENTY FOUR
BENNY AND BJORN – AFTER ABBA
AFTER CHESS

In April 1984 an exclusive interview with Bjorn appeared in England's 'News Of The World' newspaper, which coincided with the release of a special boxed set of ABBA's singles to celebrate the tenth anniversary of their Eurovision victory. During this rare and interesting interview, Bjorn talked opening about his divorce, ABBA, Eurovision and the future:

DIVORCE

"People think how lucky I must have been to be married to Agnetha. I could see men looking enviously, but it doesn't make any difference if every man in the audience is looking at your wife's body. If you don't find her attractive anymore, then that's it. People used to say that we broke up because we were in the same group and we used to see too much of each other. That's rubbish. Most of the time I would be writing or working in the studio, and she was doing something else. And we didn't spend our time in bed discussing business. What happened to us happens to a lot of relationships – we just drifted apart. We would have broken up if I had been a civil engineer and she had been a nurse. It might have lasted a little longer but the final outcome would have been exactly the same. Obviously, every couple have rows, but we were having the wrong sort of rows – the sort that you can't resolve because you no longer communicate. And when I found that I no longer wanted to go home in the evening and would try to delay it as late as possible, hoping that Agnetha would have gone to bed, then I knew that I had to do something about it."

ABBA

"We started out as friends. We were all playing with different Swedish groups, and then we found that we were more than just boyfriends and girlfriends, and it just fell into place. We worked well together because we enjoyed being together – we weren't manufacturered. We could have formed a firm of accountants, but we just happened to be musicians. Looking back, I suppose we were the ideal team – the two girls were the faces and the two boys the artists. Frankly, there was no way that people were ever going to pay eight pounds to come and see Benny and me performing. We're not good-looking enough and we're not great singers either. But we wrote the songs, and the girls were great singers and beautiful, so they sold our music. We were confident that we could do quite well, but we never expected to go sky high. I always thought that I would make it – but not that way. I expected it to be as a songwriter or producer, but not a pop star. I never really wanted to be a pop star – it just happened. At 28, you can't take yourself seriously as a pop star – I never expected to be part of a group that was taking the whole world by storm."

EUROVISION

"The overall standard of Eurovision is awful – the music is largely rubbish. And very few of them try to be original. If you listen to most of the songs, it's not 1984, they sound as though it's 1980. They create the song and sound that they think should be right for the contest, so in the end they all sound the same. I always watch it, though, because it's so bad, it's funny. If we had been English we wouldn't have competed, but being Swedish we had to. It was the only way people would take any notice of us."

THE FUTURE OF ABBA

"Certainly the first phase of ABBA is finished. I don't like to say that it's gone forever because you never know what the future holds. We may decide in a few years time that it would be fun to do a record or a few concerts, but at the moment we are all very busy with different things. You have to move on or do other things. Everyone knows that you can't have thirty years of number one records – so from where we were, the sales could only drop. At the moment none of us have any ambitions left with ABBA. It's not something that any of us will actually finish – it will merely cease to be.

Of course we were all disappointed by the failure of the last two singles, but there was a tiredness about the group, a lack of vitality. For the first time ever, we had stopped having fun recording. ABBA had got to the point where it could go no further."

In November 1984 Bjorn, Lena and their daughter, Emma , left Sweden and made a new home for themselves in England. From his new country estate in Henley-On-Thames, Bjorn said "I've been thinking about moving to England for many years. In Sweden I felt the lack of freedom and that so many decisions were taken away from me by politicians. For example, they take more than eighty per cent of income in tax. It wasn't that the remaining twenty per cent wouldn't have been enough, it was the fact that I couldn't make my own decisions about what to do with my own money. Now I feel more international than either British or Swedish. My roots are certainly in Europe but it doesn't make much difference where I am. My security is with me and my family."

'GEMINI' by Gemini (Anders and Karin Glenmark)

'Slowly'	*(Benny Andersson/Bjorn Ulvaeus)*
'Too Much Love Is Wasted"	*(Benny Andersson/Bjorn Ulvaeus)*
'Slow Emotion'	*(Benny Andersson/Bjorn Ulvaeus)*
'Just Like That'	*(Benny Andersson/Bjorn Ulvaeus)*
'Falling'	*(Benny Andersson/Bjorn Ulvaeus)*
'Have Mercy'	*(Benny Andersson/Bjorn Ulvaeus)*
'Live On Love'	*(Benny Andersson/Bjorn Ulvaeus)*
'In The Middle Of Nowhere'	*(Benny Andersson/Bjorn Ulvaeus)*
'Another You Another Me'	*(Benny Andersson/Bjorn Ulvaeus)*

During 1985 Benny and Bjorn took a break from 'Chess' activties to produce the debut album for Swedish borther-and-sister-duo 'Gemini'. As well as producing the album, Benny and Bjorn also contributed six of the album's ten songs. "Benny and I were dying to make a new pop album" said Bjorn. "We haven't worked on one since ABBA's last album in 1981. Since then 'Chess' and 'Gemini' have taken over our lives." The album was recorded at Polar Music Studios, Stockholm, and was the first release for Benny's new production company – Mono Music AB. At the international launch of the album, Benny said "Obviously some people will recognise Bjorn's and my way of writing songs – but this is not a new ABBA."

With the release of the album and single, 'Just Like That', Gemini embarked on a promotional tour of Europe accompanied by Benny, who also appeared on various television shows with them. "Benny and Bjorn have opened doors for us" said Karin Glenmark, ". . . and to be compared with ABBA is very flattering, but I feel our sound is different."

Throughout Scandanavia the album and single were an immediate success; however, elsewhere throughout Europe sales were varied and mainly poor. Despite the input from Benny and Bjorn, Gemini failed to achieve the success and recognition they had hoped for.

During the first five months of 1986, Benny and Bjorn were very much preoccupied with activities surrounding the London premiere of 'Chess'. However, on 1st May Bjorn became a father once again when Lena gave birth to a healthy baby girl. Therefore, after the premiere of 'Chess' on 14th May, both Benny and Bjorn spent the remainder of the year at home with their families.

'GEMINISM' by Gemini

'T.L.C.'	*(Benny Andersson/Bjorn Ulvaeus)*
'Beat The Heat'	*(Anders Glenmark/Ingela Forsman)*
'Mio My Mio'	*(Benny Andersson./Bjorn Ulvaeus)*
'Ghost Town'	*(Benny Andersson/Bjorn Ulvaeus)*
'I Am The Universe'	*(Benny Andersson/Bjorn Ulvaeus)*
'Sniffin' Out The Snakes'	*(Anders Glenmark/Ingela Forsman)*
'I'm A Bitch When I See Red'	*(Benny Andersson/Bjorn Ulvaeus)*
'There's No Way To Fool A Heart'	*(Benny Andersson/Ingela Forsman)*
'Wild About That Girl'	*(Anders Glenmark/Bjorn Ulvaeus/Dan Sundqvist)*
'Nearly There'	*(Benny Andersson/Bjorn Ulvaeus)*

The beginning of 1987 saw Benny and Bjorn working with Gemini once again on their second album – 'Geminism'. Recorded at Polar Studios, Stockholm, Benny and Bjorn contributed and produced six of the album's ten songs, with Benny producing the remaining four songs with Anders Glenmark. When released in April by Benny's production company, Mono Music, 'Geminism' soon made a big impact on the Swedish charts. But elsewhere in Europe its success was very limited. In England the album was not released at all.

For the remainder of 1987, Benny and Bjorn continued writing. Together with Anders Eljas, Benny composed the soundtrack to a Swedish children's film, 'Mio Min Mio', which was a great success with Swedes of all ages. Then Benny and Bjorn together wrote a 'classical' song, titled 'Klinga Mina Klocker' ('Ring My Bell'), which they recorded in October at Polar Music Studios, Stockholm, with the Swedish Radio Symphony Orchestra and a host of well-known Swedish singers – including Frida. When released throughout Sweden, 'Klinga Mina Klockor' was nominated for, and later won, a Swedish 'Grammy' award.

During the first few months of 1988, Benny and Bjorn were once again involved with 'Chess' and the Broadway production of the show. However, upon his return to Stockholm, Benny returned to his musical 'roots' and produced a 'folk' album featuring various Swedish folk artists. The album, titled 'Orsa Spelman', featured fifteen songs, of which Benny played the accordian and synthesizer on nine songs.

During 1989 Benny wrote, produced and recorded his very first solo album, titled 'November 1989'. Recorded by Benny at his own recording studio, Mono Music Studio, the album featured ten 'instrumental' songs together with the latest 'classical' Andersson/Ulvaeus composition titled 'The Conductor', performed by Tommy Korberg. The album was released throughout Scandanavia only, in November (hence the album's title), and was an immediate hit with the audience and critics alike.

'November 1989' received much acclaim throughout Sweden and, in February 1990, Benny was awarded a Swedish 'Grammy' for the album.

In April 1989, England's 'Guitarist' magazine published an exclusive interview with Bjorn conducted by Tony Hicks, from the group 'The Hollies'. During the interview Bjorn talked about his career to date, and when asked "Do you think you'll ever do anything with ABBA again?', Bjorn replied, "Well . . . I can see us coming together again. I don't know for what reason, but if there is a motivation . . . I mean, I thought the sound of the two girls together was a very good sound, and we have songs that we write now that I would like to hear with ABBA. These songs we have not recorded at all – they're just there."

During 1990 Benny produced two albums. The first was a second 'folk' album, titled 'Fiolen Min', which again featured various Swedish 'folk' artists. Recorded at Mono Music Studio, the album featured twenty folk songs, of which Benny played the accordian and synthesizer on six songs. The second album Benny produced was for the Swedish 'girl' group 'The Ainsbusk Singers', titled 'More Armore', which was recorded at Mono Music Studio. Benny also wrote the single release from the album, titled 'Lassie' which, when released spent four weeks at the top of the Swedish charts.

Also during 1990 Benny and Bjorn wrote and produced the theme tune for the 1990 World Equestrian Games, which were held in Stockholm. The song, titled, 'Upp Till Kamp' was sung by Tommy Korberg.

The beginning of 1991 saw Bjorn move back to Stockholm with his family so that he could begin writing a new musical together with Benny. The musical is based on Willhelm Moberg's novel 'The Immigrants', described by Bjorn as "One of the greatest and most important novels in the Swedish language". Despite spending the majority of 1991 working on their new musical, Benny and Bjorn took a short break to write a song, titled 'Beatrice', for Swedish singer Kalle Moraeus. Benny and Bjorn were also 'session' musicians when Kalle recorded her song at Polar Music Studios.

"I thought the sound of the two girls together was a very good sound, and we have songs that we write now that I would like to hear with ABBA. These songs we have not recorded at all – they're just there."

CHAPTER TWENTY FIVE
AGENTHA STANDS ALONE

It was during the summer of 1982 that Agnetha took the first step to renew here solo career, after working with ABBA for more than ten years. For her first solo project, Agnetha not only diversified, but, at the same time, realised her long-held ambition to act when she accepted her first character role in a Swedish move 'Raskenstram'. "It's about a Swedish Casanova, and it's taken from reality – his name was Raskenstam," said Agnetha. "He was a man who lived in Sweden, and during the 40's he was engaged with over a hundred women at the same time. I happen to be one of the women, but one very important one, because I play the woman that he really loved and got two children with. He wa a terrible man, I must say, he cheated the ladies out of money and so on . . ." Wnen 'Raskenstam' received its premiere in Stockholm on August 19th 1983, both the film and Agnetha's performance were critically acclaimed. Talking about here movie debut, Agnetha said "I've always been interested in making films and somewhere deep inside I've had this feeling that I'm able to act. When I first read the manuscript to 'Raskenstam' I knew that I could make Lisa, and it was a fantastic experience to do something new and to succeed – I liked it a lot – it was very exciting to try. What I like about acting is that you create something in one or two minutes, it's what happens then, what comes out, and I like that challenge."

'WRAP YOUR ARMS AROUND ME'

'The Heat Is On'	(Florrie Palmer/Tony Ashton)
'Can't Shake Loose'	(Russ Ballard)
'Shame'	(David Clark Allen)
'Stay'	(David Clark Allen)
'Once Burned, Twice Shy'	(Dan Tyler/Richard Spady Brannan)
'Mr. Persausion'	(Susan Lynch/Larry Whitman)
'Wrap Your Arms Around Me'	(Mike Chapman/Holly Knight)
'To Love'	(Jill Brandt/Randy Goodrum)
'I Wish Tonight Could Last Forever'	(Russ Ballard)
'Man'	(Angetha Faltskog)
'Take Good Care Of Your Children'	(Tomas Ledin)
'Stand By My Side'	(Guido + Maurizli de Engelis/David Cowles)

On January 20th 1983 Agnetha began recording her first English-language solo album at Polar Music Studios, Stockholm. For her first international solo ablum, Agnetha had chosen as her producer Mike Chapman, who had already established himself as one of the world's leading producers through his work with Blondie, Sweet, Smokie and Suzy Quatro. Together with Mike, Agnetha had chosen all the songs for her album and had also employed a team of musicians to play on the album.

Many of the musicians, with the exception of Chris Norman, Alan Silson and Terry Uttley from 'Smokie', were already familiar to Agnetha, as they had worked with her in ABBA – Bass: Rutger Gunnarsson, Guitars: Lasse Wellander, Drums: Per Lindvall, Keyboards: Peter Ljung, Percussion: Ake Sungvist, Accordian & Saxophones: Kajtek Wojciechowski, Harmonica: Mats Ronander, Harp: Ingegerd Fredlund, Strings: Swedish Radio Symphony Orchestra, Backing Vocals: Smokie, Berit Andersson, Maritza Horn, Diana Nunez, Agnetha, Engineer: Michael B Tretow.

By April 'Wrap Your Arms Around Me' was complete so Agnetha turned her attentions to promotional activities, and began talking about her new album:

"I like to sing everything – I like to sing rock and I like to sign ballads, and I think in this album the material is very varied."

"We started to work with the material for the album, listening to different cassettses, last autumn, both Mike Chapman and I, and Stikkan Anderson. There were a lot of cassettes coming in with very good songs, so I think we had twenty songs in the beginning and then we had to cut it down to twelve. I must say I am very, very pleased with the sound and the material and the songs that we picked . . ."

". . . We said from the start that there have to be good melodies, because that's very important, I think. We also said from the start that it was going to be a very positive album, with a warm atmosphere – and I think that we have succeeded. I had a wonderful time working on this album. Mike has revealed a lot of new sides within myself. I do not want to say my voice is getting better and better, but it is getting stronger and more expressive and, compared to my first records, the difference is enormous. I really love to work in the studio.,"

Mike – "Agnetha really lets her hair down on this album."
Agnetha – "You mean, I really stick my neck out".

During May and June, 'Wrap Your Arms Around Me' was released worldwide, together with the single 'The Heat Is On'. With the release of the album and single, Agnetha embarked on an intensive promotional tour of Scandanavia, England, France, Holland and Germany. On August 22nd Agnetha also arrived in New York for seven days's promotion in America. As well as her numerous television appearances in the countries that she visited, Agnetha made her own TV Special in Stockholm, in which she performed six songs from her album. Commercially, both 'Wrap Your Arms Around Me' and 'The Heat Is On' did very well and both achieved Top Twenty positions in the territories where they were released. Total sales of the album and single exceeded two million copies. In American 'Can't Shake Loose' was chosen as the single release and soon earned Agnetha her first American solo hit – it peaked at number-five on the Billboard charts.

Critically, 'Wrap Your Arms Around Me' was less well received: 'Wrap Your Arms Around Me', despite some pleasant moments, not only fails to find any new revelation in Agnetha's talent, but it isn't even as interesting as an ABBA album. Neither the material nor the sound of this record force Agnetha to tap anything in her range of expression" wrote Record Magazine, whilst American's Rolling Stone commented: "As a tireless booster of ABBA, it grieves me greatly to report what a disappointment Agnetha Faltskog's first solo album is. 'Wrap Your Arms Around Me' is a treacley, string-sopped outing that doesn't begin to do her justice."

On September 30th Agnetha arrived in England in order to promote her new single release, 'Can't Shake Loose'. However, if Agnetha could have forseen the forthcoming events, she would most probably have decided to stay at home. Firstly, during her television appearance on Noel Edmonds' 'Late Late Breakfast Show', Agnetha fell down some steps on stage and cut her elbow. Then, whilst travelling back home to Sweden on Sunday 2nd October, she was involved in an accident when her driver lost control of her coach, causing it to overturn. Luckily, nobody was seriously injured; but Agnetha spent the night in hospital in Southern Sweden, where she received treatment for shock, cuts and bruises. Ironically, on her last promotional visit to England in May, Agnetha had told BBC radio presenter, Gloria Hunniford, that her fear of flying meant that she now only travelled by bus and boat:

"Is it true that you won't fly?"
"Oh, I'm scared of it – we go by bus and boat on this trip."

"Do you always go by bus and boat?"
"No, no, I've been flying a lot for fifteen years, all over the world, but in a way I never get used to it – I can't accept it. It's not a natural way of travelling, I think. What's scary is that you can't do anything about it if something happens – when you go by road you think you can handle it in another way, so now that I have a choice I will travel by bus and boat."

Towards the end of 1983, Agnetha released a new single exclusively in Sweden . The single featured two songs from the soundtrack of a Swedish movie titled 'P&B'. When released, the single – 'It's So Nice To Be Rich/'P&B' – topped the Swedish charts and so brought to an end Agnetha's first and highly successful years as an international solo artiste.

During 1984 Agnetha stayed very much out of the public eye, spending much of her time at home, relaxing with her children. However, in May Agentha hosted a Swedish TV Special – 'Jonkopingsyra', which celebrated the 700th anniversary of her hometown, Jonkoping. Being Jonkoping's most successful and famous citizen, Agnetha received a wam welcome from the city's people. The highlight of the show for Agnetha, came when a children's choir, conducted by Agnetha's old music teacher, sang a selection of her pre-ABBA solo songs. During the second half of 1984, Agnetha began making preparations for her second, English-language, solo album. For the latest album, Agnetha had chosen Eric Stewart, from the British Group 10cc, to produce her, and together they began choosing songs for their musical collaboration.

"I've been flying a lot for fifteen years, all over the world, but in a way I never get used to it – I can't accept it."

A168A

A169A

'EYES OF A WOMAN'

'One Way Love'	*(Jeff Plane)*
'Eyes Of A Woman'	*(Paris Edvinson/Marianne Flynner)*
'Just One Heart'	*(Paul Muggleton/Robert Noble)*
'I Won't Let You Go'	*(Agnetha Faltskog/Eric Stewart)*
'The Angels Cry'	*(Justin Hayward)*
'Click Track'	*(Janice & Phil Palmer)*
'We Should Be Together'	*(Jay Gruska/Tom Keane)*
'I Won't Be Leaving You'	*(Eric Stewart)*
'Save Me (Why Don't You)'	*(Eric Stewart)*
'I Keep Turning Off Lights'	*(China Burton)*
'We Move As One'	*(John Wetton/Geoff Downes)*

B-SIDE TRACKS:

'You're There'	*(Agnetha Faltskog/Eric Stewart)*
'Turn The World Around'	*(Randy Edleman)*

In January 1985, Agnetha began recording her second English-language solo album at Polar Music Studios, Stockholm, together with a team of Swedish and British musicians:

Drums: Jamie Lane, Bass: Rutger Gunnarsson, Guitars: Rick Fenn, Justin Hayward, Keyboards: Vic Ermson, Percussion: Eric Stewart, Backing Vocals: Anders & Karin Glenmark, Marianne Flynner, Eric Stewart, Agnetha. Engineered and mixed by Paris Edvinson.

During the last week of March Agnetha released her self-penned song, 'I Won't Let You Go' as her new single, which was followed by the release of her album, 'Eyes Of A Woman', the following week. Throughout Europe both the single and the album made an immediate impact on the charts, and sales were very good. In America, 'Eyes Of A Woman' was not released although a remixed version of 'One Way Love' was released as a limited 12-inch single and became a big 'dance' hit on the American club scene.

With the release of her new album and single, Agnetha centred her promotional activities around her appearance at the Montreux Pop Festival and a half-hour TV Special. In the TV Special, filmed in Stockholm and called 'A For Agnetha', Agnetha performed five songs from her album and also talked about her life, past and present:

"For more than ten years I was one of the members of ABBA and hounded by the press and fans everywhere I went. Now I have started to walk my own way – to take the first steps of my own solo career – I'm going to see if I can fly on my own."

Agnetha sings 'One Way Love'

"I started to sing when I was 15 years old, touring Sweden with a dance band. We played hotels and dance halls in the wintertime, and during the summer we'd play the very special Swedish people's parks. God, I must have played hundreds of these places, where people come out in the light summer nights to dance and have a good time in the open air . . ."

". . . I had learned how to take hold of an audience in those first tough years, and I still remember how nervous I was when Daddy and I took the train to Stockholm for the first time. I was still only seventeen, and still a country girl."

Agnetha sings 'Just One Heart'

"I was lucky from the beginning in the big city. I met Bjorn, Benny and Frida in the late Sixties. We became close to each other and created ABBA. In 1974 we won the Eurovision Song Contest in Brighton, and I used to say that was how the ten crazy years started. I had no idea of what was coming and I don't think I could go through it again. I gave birth to two children during those years and, to this day, I don't really know how I managed to keep up with everything. Many times I have felt like a stranger in many places, and often I just wanted to go home again – to be alone – but the show had to go on."

Agnetha sings 'We Should Be Together'

"Today, I have to work so that I feel satisfied with myself and what I'm doing. I wrote all my own material when I started on my own as a teenager, but during the ABBA years Bjorn and Benny wrote all the songs. I still try to compose, but to be really good, to come up with something really original, is very hard work and requires a lot of discipline, at least in my case. But I think it's fun to have one or two of my own songs on my albums, so I continue. I can have problems with the English lyrics sometimes, so that's how my friend, Eric Stewart, came to write them for this song."

Agnetha sings 'I Won't Let You Go'

"After all I've been through, I feel that I've learned a lot from life, as an artist and as a mother. It's been tough sometimes, but I've learned one thing; I don't have to waste my time on superficial things any longer. I hate cocktail parties where people are smiling and making contacts and deals without really getting to know each other."

Agnetha sings 'Click Track'

"It's hard to think that I could live anywhere else but here in Sweden. The climate is hard sometimes, but isn't it also beautiful? I have all my family and relatives here; my parents, my children and my friends. I believe you have to take care of your real friends. How many deep and close friends can one have in a lifetime? Three or four, not many more. I'm interested in what's going on in the world – the injustice can make me sad and angry. I really feel ashamed and desperate when I think of all the mothers in the world who don't have milk to give their babies. I see my own kids worrying about the arms race and nuclear war, and the pollution of the earth. Will there be clean air for them to breathe? Will the earth survive? Kids think about that all the time. I want my kids to grow up as good and secure people who understand that we can, and must, always talk to each other. At least that could be a start in our attempt to solve our problems. I want my kids to feel the security that they and all other kids deserve. That is important."

Agnetha sings 'We Move As One'

After the successful release of Eyes Of A Woman, Agnetha decided to take a break from her career in order to spend time out of the public eyes, with her family. In June the Swedish newspaper 'Expressen' printed Agnetha's final interview:

"I've been on the road since 1968 and I feel that my strength is failing. I've done my part for now. Perhaps I could make myself a name in the U.S.A. but then I'd have to go there and work purposefully for at least one year, and I don't want to do that. Do you think that I'll miss the stress and the pressure? Never! . . ."

". . . On the other hand, I do not regret my involvement with ABBA for a second. ABBA meant ten years of everything that's hard for me. Ten years of being away from home, living in hotels, flying, leaving the children behind and performing. But at the same time it was very funny of course, and I am enormously grateful for our big success. It's still a great honour to write autographs and it's a wonderful feeling when new stars, whom I hardly know, tell me that they liked ABBA. When I started my solo career, however, everything was much easier. I could be myself and work in my own way. There was no need to compromise. I'm full of self-criticism and I know that I'm no good on stage, so why perform? But I've always wanted to sing. As a child I used to listen to singers like Connie Francis and Rita Pavone. I played their records over and over again, trying to act like them in front of the mirror. Many times I dreamed of being a star, but I could never imagine myself being part of such a great success as I've been through with ABBA.
When I entered the 'Phillips Studio' and I heard the orchestra playing my own song, "I Was So In Love', I didn't know what to say or where to go. It was a very special moment in my life and I will never forget it."

"Other sepcial moments?"

"When I met Bjorn and we got married and started to sing together. And when ABBA won the Eurovision Song Contest 1974, of course. But after that it was different, I never felt that dizzy feeling of happiness again. It's not that we were blasé with our success, but perhaps a little bit spoiled. It became a habit that every single we released topped the charts in England. Of course we were proud and happy every time, but as I said, it became a habit. And what's a habit can easily become a routine. Man needs challenges."

"Why do you dislike being called ABBA-Agnetha?"

"I don't like labels. I hate it. I've got my own name and my own identity."

You live a 'normal' Swedish life. Has success changed you?

"No, I don't think so. I'm not suitable to be a star. I just get embarrassed when people bow, etc."

"You must be the only person in 'Rock' who hasn't experienced drugs."

"No, many haven't done that. At concerts, Frida and I used to joke when we smelt 'grass' that we should take a deep breath before entering the stage, but I hate drugs."

'Do you think you have a reputation as a 'stupid blonde'?"

'Not so much, more like a fragile person who doesn't know what to do. I live in my own world but I'm very observant of what happens around me. I've got intuition and I'm a strong woman. Just because I'm frightened of flying everyone seems to think that I'm frightened of everything. The media wants you to have opinions about everything, but I don't have answers for everything."

'You spend a lot of time with your children."

'Yes, very much. That is very importat to me. They need me even more now that Bjorn has moved to London."

'What do you think about Bjorn moving to London?"

'I don't understand it. He's got strong reasons, but I don't think that it can be so important that you can leave your children. It's more trouble for the children to see him."

'How did they react?"

'They have calmed down now. They never liked to be thrown between me and Bjorn. It's tough for children to have two homes, but now they can feel safe and secure with me."

After just over a year of silence, towards the end of 1986 Agnetha began making plans to resume her recording career. On November 10th 1986, Agnetha released a new single, a duet with fellow-Swede, Ola hakansson, titled 'The Way You Are'/'Fly Like The Eagle'. Both songs were from the Swedish film 'It's Time For Sweden' and Agnetha had recorded them earlier in the year at Sonet Studios, Stockholm. The single was also Agnetha's first release for her own production company – Agnetha Falskog Productions AB. Throughout Sweden, Agnetha and Ola performed the song on a few television programmes, which resulted in the single becoming a Top Ten hit. But throughout Europe the unexpected release of the single, together with a lack of promotion, meant that the single made very little impression on the charts. As 1986 came to a close, Agnetha signed a new recording contract with WEA Records Ltd, and was looking forward to 1987 when she would resume her recording career.

After recording a 'Christmas album' together with her daughter, Linda, in November 1980, the beginning of 1987 saw Agnetha recording a 'children's album' together with her ten-year old son, Christian. The album, titled 'Kom Folj Med I Var Karusell' ('Come Ride In Our Carousel'), was recorded at Sonet Studios 2, Stockholm and contained sixteen children's song. The album was also produced by Agnetha, together with Michael B. Tretow. "I'm lucky to have been able to work on albums with both my children" said Agnetha. 'However, I don't suppose either one of them will pursue a muscial career. Linda has been spending much of her time competing in horse jumping while Christian is a very good painter." When released throughout Sweden the album, together with the accompanying single 'Pa Sondag' ('On Sunday'), did very well and proved to be a great success with Swedes of all ages.

'I STAND ALONE'

'The Last Time'	*(Robin Randall, Judithe Randall, Jeff Law)*
'Little White Secrets'	*(Ellen Schwartz, Roger Bruno, Susan Pomerantz)*
'I Wasn't The One' (Who Said Goodbye)	*(Mark Mueller, Aaron Zigman)*
'Love In A World Gone Mad'	*(Billy Livsey, Pete Singfield)*
'Maybe It Was Magic'	*(Peter Brown, Pat Hurley)*
'Let It Shine'	*(Austin Roberts, Bill LaBounty, Beckie Foster)*
'We Got A Way'	*(John Robinson, Franne Golde, Martin Walsh)*
'I Stand Alone'	*(Peter Cetera, Bruce Gaitsch)*
'Are You Gonna Throw It All Away?'	*(Dainne Warren, Albert Hammond, Guy Roche)*
'If You Need Somebody Tonight'	*(Dainne Warren, Albert Hammond)*

It was during a Red Cross-sponsored telethon in Stockholm 1986 that Agnetha first me the producer of her third English-language solo album – American singer/songwriter, Peter Cetera. During their first meeting Peter suggested to Agnetha that someday they should work together. However, in the beginning was very sceptical, "You meet so many people in this business who are well-intentioned, but schedules and commitments often prevent these kind of projects from materialising" said Agnetha. "However, to my surprise Peter and I started transAtlantic communications about the project soon after we met and we never let the idea die."

Three months later, after formally agreeing to go ahead with the project, Peter returned to Stockholm to work with Agnetha on song selections. During the Spring of 1987 Agnetha began recording her album but, for the first time in her career, Agnetha recorded not in Sweden but in America, at the Chartmaker Studios, Malibu, California. "Peter and the co-producer, Bruce Gaitsch, wanted to do it there because they were used to the studios and the musicians – so it was better" said Agnetha.

The musicians, all new to Agnetha but fondly referred to by her as 'The Inner Circle', were: Guitars + Synthesizer programming: Bruce Gaitsch, Drums: John Robinson, Keyboards: Randy Waldman, Synthesizers, bells and whistles: Robbie Buchanan, Percussion: Paulinho Da Gosta, Bass: Neil Stubenhaus, Saxophone: David Boruff, Harmonica: Tommy Morgan, Backing Vocals: Kenny Cetera, Darlene Koldenhoven, Linda Harmon, Agnetha and Peter, Engineer: Rick Holbrook.

After spending five weeks in America recording her album, Agnetha began talking about her latest musical collaboration:

"I'm very critical of my own writing and I like to take a long time on my songs, carefully constructing the melodies and thinking for quite a while about the lyrics. In order to accommodate the schedules of all involved, we needed to select the songs and begin laying down basic tracks for the album almost as soon as we have decided to go ahead with the project. And so I really had no time to compose, but I made extra efforts to select songs that relfect my true emotions. In that respect, my favourite songs on the album are 'Let It Shine', 'I Wasn't The One' and 'I Stand Alone.' When I hear a song I get a lot of ideas about how a song should sound on record, with all sorts of harmonies and sounds developing in my head. I like to add those contributions in the studio, and Peter was very receptive to my ideas. It was great to work with Peter. He was so careful with the vocal tracks, he's so sensitive, and has a really good ear. It was a great challenge for me to work with him, since I've been an admirer of his music for such a long time. I wanted my work to live up to his standards. For my next musical project, I only hope I can find another challenge as big as this one was."

On November 9th, 'I Stand Alone' was released throughout Sweden only and soon topped the album charts, selling 170,000 copies. To coincide with the album's release, Agnetha appeared on Swedish TV, where she was interviewed by Jacob Dahlin and also performed four songs from 'I Stand Alone'.

On Janaury 15th, 'I Stand Alone' was released worldwide, together with the single 'The Last Time'. Throughout Europe both the album and the single were well received by the critics and the audience and both made an immediate impact on the charts. Total sales for the album and single once again approached two million copies. During the first week of February, Agnetha arrived in England for a short promotional visit. Her only television appearance was on the BBC chat show 'Wogan', where she was given a rapturous welcome from the studio audience. Agnetha also met the British press and, during her numerous interviews, talked about her life today and reflected upon her career:

"I am now doing what I always wanted to do – writing songs, singing and recording, and being a little star. I like being a little star – being a big star is too much pressure and I don't like pressure at all. I really don't miss all the fame and success of ABBA. We worked so hard for such a long time – we travelled the world. but in almost every place we visited, it was work, work, work and we didn't have the chance to see anything. I've been to many places but I've no idea what they were about because we were working all the time – always in a rush. But we are all very proud of what we achieved. I don't blame ABBA for the break-up of my and Bjorn's marriage. I have no guilty feelings and that goes for all of us. Bjorn and I would have split anyway – we just grew away from each other. But, we are still good friend. I wouldn't mind marrying again. The press in Sweden write a lot of bad things about me. Some newspapers have been writing that I am more or less hiding in my house all the time, like Greta Garbo, but that's not the case at all. I go out every day with my dog for long walks, it's just tht people don't recognise me. I look very normal. The Swedish press think that I am too normal. Maybe I want to be a little mysterious, like Garbo. I don't want to be an open book, so people know everything about me. Who wants that? but I don't have anything to hide either. I'm very happy at the moment. I have a lot of friends, new friends, female and male – I feel good. Your certainly shouldn't think of me as a lonely blonde, living in Sweden – That would be totally wrong."

Since 1988, Agnetha has remained away from the music busines and has devoted herself to her family and children. On Saturday 15th December 1990, Agnetha married a 44-year-old Swedish surgeon, Tomas Sonnenfeld, who works at Stockholm's Huddinge Hospital. The wedding ceremony took place at the Chruch of Ekero near Agnetha's home, just outside Stockholm, amid great secrecy. Only a few close friends and relations attended. The Swedish press knew nothing about the wedding until a small announcement appeared in the Swedish newspaper Dagens Nyheter the following day. When the news of Agnetha's wedding broke, there was a blaze of publicity throughout Sweden and the Swedish newspaper 'Expressen' went to Agnetha's home in the hope of talking to the newly-weds. However, Agnetha's daughter, Linda, was the only person to talk to the press and said "They have relaxed all day and will spend the next few days at home, in private."

However, Agnetha and Tomas's marriage was not to last, and in early 1993, both began divorce proceedings. Agnetha's daughter, Linda, has now moved from home, and is living in her own flat in central Stockholm. Agnetha remains at home with her son, Christian.

Today, Agnetha still seems to remain reluctant to continue with her music career – but who knows?

CHAPTER TWENTY SIX
THE DREAM IS STILL ALIVE

It is now twenty years since Agnetha Faltskog, Benny Andersson, Bjorn Ulvaeus and Anni-Frid Lyngstad, launched themselves to a worldwide audience, as ABBA, when they won the 1974 Eurovision Song Contest in Brighton. It is also twelve years since ABBA ceased to record together.

The nineties have seen a mass resurrection of interest and appreciation of ABBA – confirming beyond all doubt their position as one of the top five acts of all time.

For five years, Australian ABBA impersonators Bjorn Again, have enjoyed success performing ABBA songs to sell-out audiences throughout the world – most recently at London's Royal Albert Hall. "I'm a bit offended that Bjorn Again impersonate us in a dialect that resembles the Swedish chef in The Muppets", says Bjorn, " But if they'd take that away, then fine - the best of luck to them." In June 1992, British band Erasure released their 'Abba-esque EP', featuring cover versions of four ABBA songs. This release topped the singles charts in territories all around the world.

"The pop charts haven't been the same since the demise of ABBA", said Andy Bell from Erasure, "It was the first time that I'd heard gorgeous harmonies and angelic choruses. I loved the fact that when ABBA went on to make disco – like Voulez Vous - they really understood it." Also during 1992, Irish band U2 paid their own tribute to ABBA by Performing 'Dancing Queen' throughout their 'ZOOTV World Tour', and on June 11th they were joined on stage by Benny and Bjorn at the Stockholm concert. "We are very flattered" said Bjorn, "Most groups who stopped ten years ago are forgotten now."

On August 24th 1992, Polygram released the first ABBA single for ten years - 'Dancing Queen', which was an immediate international hit. This was followed on September 28th by a compilation album, 'ABBA Gold', featuring nineteen classic tracks. This was also chartbound, hitting the number one spot, and achieved Platinum status in over twenty different countries. Within six months, sales had topped an amazing four and a half million. With this renewed popularity, rumours of a reunion were rife. But Bjorn quickly dismissed such speculation, " When we split up in 1982, that was it. And that is how it is going to stay. I don't believe in making any half-assed comebacks. I think that it is so pathetic when old bands who have broken-up, go back on the road again. We still have a lot of credibility, and that's the way I want it to stay."

But Bjorn did announce that he was getting together with Benny to work on an album with a 23 year old Swedish singer, Josephin Nilsson. The album was to be written by the pair, and produced at Polar Music Studios by Benny. The album, 'Shapes', was eventually released in April 1993, and featured ten new Andersson/Ulvaeus compositions. 'Heaven And Hell' was taken off the album as Nilsson's debut single, and true to form, was soon sitting on top of the Swedish singles chart. Bjorn and Benny still had that magic.

On May 24th, 'MORE ABBA GOLD' was released, and like it's predecessor made an immediate impact on album charts around the globe. And once again the subject of a reunion was in the forefront of people's minds, and so Bjorn was back in the spotlight: "We sold a lot of records, so when the 70's revival happened, back came ABBA. But I still feel far away from it all. I realise that millions of records are being sold out there, and that it has something to do with me, but I still feel removed from it: it was another time, and I was another person. But it is still very flattering that our music is still around."

On July 20th, BBC Television screened their ABBA TV special throughout England, as part of an ABBA tribute night. 'A For ABBA' featured 'classic' ABBA television appearances, alongside a string of vocal, comical, and musical tributes. Among those featured were: U2, Erasure, Bjorn Again, Elvis Costello, Tim Rice, and Ray Davies of The Kinks. Benny and Bjorn also made an appearance, by satellite from Stockholm, at the end of the programme. They mused about their recent renewed popularity, and Benny commented: "We were extremely corny, I think. We never thought about the clothes and our general style. And all that rubbish about being 'bigger than Volvo', and being 'paid in oil' – we can laugh about it now. I think that it is fantastic that our music is still around, and that they didn't kill us for being so corny!"

Whatever the future may hold for Agnetha, Benny, Bjorn, and Frida, ABBA's position in popular culture is carved in stone. The music still goes on . . .

DISCOGRAPHY

ABBA SINGLE RELEASES

1972 People Need Love/Merry Go Round
1972 He Is Your Brother/Santa Rosa
1973 Love Isn't Easy/I Am Just A Girl
1973 Ring Ring (Swedish version)/Ah Vilka Tider
1973 Ring Ring (English version)/Merry Go Round
1974 Waterloo (Swedish version)/Honey Honey *(Swedish version)*
1974 Waterloo (English version)/Watch Out
1974 Honey Honey/King Kong Song
1974 So Long/I've Been Waiting For You
1975 I Do I Do I Do I Do I Do/Rock Me
1975 SOS/Man In The Middle
1975 Mamma Mia/Tropical Loveland
1976 Fernando/Hey Hey Helen
1976 Dancing Queen/That's Me
1976 Money Money Money/Crazy World
1977 Knowing Me Knowing You/Happy Hawaii
1977 The Name OF The Game/I Wonder (Departure) *(Live version)*
1977 Take A Chance On Me/I'm A Marionett
1977 Eagle/Thank-You for The Music
1978 Summer Night City/Medley
1979 Chiquitita/Lovelight
1979 Does Your Mother Know/Kisses of Fire
1979 Voulez Vous/Angeleyes
1979 Gimmie Gimmie Gimmie (A Man After Midnight)/The King Has Lost His Crown
1979 I Have A Dream/Take A Chance On Me *(Live version)*
1980 The Winner Takes It All/Elaine
1980 Super Trouper/The Piper
1981 Lay All Your Love On Me/On And On And On *(12" release only)*
1981 One Of Us/Should I Laugh or Cry
1981 One Of Us/Should I Laugh or Cry *(Limited picture disc release)*
1982 Head Over Heels/The Visitors
1982 The Day Before Your Came/Cassandra
1982 Under Attack/You Owe Me One
1982 Under Attack/You Owe Me One   *(Limited picture disc release)*
1983 Thank-You For The Music/Our Last Summer
1992 Dancing Queen/Lay All Your Love On Me E.P.
1992 Voulez Vous/Summer Night City E.P.
1992 Thank-You For The Music/Happy New Year E.P.

ABBA ALBUM RELEASES

1973 Ring Ring
1974 Waterloo
1975 ABBA
1975 Greatest Hits Vol 1
1976 Arrival
1977 The Album
1979 Voulez Vous
1979 Voulez Vous (*Limited picture disc release*)
1979 Greatest Hits Vol 2
1980 Gracias Por La Muscia
1980 Super Trouper
1981 The Visitors
1982 The Singles – The First Ten Years
1983 Thank-You for the Music
1986 Live
1992 GOLD
1993 MORE ABBA GOLD

ABBA BOX SETS

1980 Super Trouper
1982 The Singles – The First Ten Years
1984 The Anniversary Singles Collection
1984 The Singles Collection

AGNETHA FALTSKOG SINGLE RELEASES

1967 Folj Med Mig/Jag Var Sa Kar
1969 Slutet Gott Alting Gott/Utan Dej Mitt Liv Gar Vidare
1968 En Sommar Med Dej/Forsonade
1968 Den Jan Vantat Pa/Alting Har Forandrat Sig
1968 Robinson Crusoe/Sonny Boy (*German release only*)
1968 Senor Gonzales/Mein Schonster Tag (*German release only*)
1969 Sjung Denna Sang/Nagonting hander Med Mej
1969 Fram for Svenska Sommaen/Eng Gang Fanns Bara Vi Tva
1969 Tag Min Hand Lat Oss Bli Vanner/Hjartat Kronprins
1969 Zigenavan/Som En Vind Kom Du Till Mej
1969 Skal Kara Van/Det Handler Om Karlek
1969 Concerto D'Amore/Wie Der Wind (*German release only*)
1969 Wer Schreibt heut Noch Liebesbriefe?/Das Fest Der Pompadour (*German release only*)
1969 Fragenzeichen Mag Ich Nicht/Wie Der Nachste Autobus (*German release only*)
1970 Om Tarar Vore Guld/Litet Solskensbam
1970 Som Ett Eko/Ta Det Bara Med Ro
1970 Ein Kleiner Mann In Einer Flasche/Ich Suchte Leibe Bei Dir (*German release only*)
1971 Kungens Vaktparad/Jag Vill Att Du Skall Bli Lycklig
1971 Manga Ganger An/Han Lamnar Mig For Att Komma Till Dig
1971 Nya Ord/Drom Ar Drom Och Saga Saga
1972 Vart Ska Min Karlek Fora/Nu Skall Bli Du Stilla
1972 Tio Mil Kvar Till Korpilombolo/Sa Glad Som Dina Ogon

1972 Geh Mitt Cott/Tausend Wunder *(German release only)*
1972 Komm Doch Zu Mir/Ich Denk' An Dich *(German release only)*
1973 Vi Har Hunnit Fram Till Regrangen/En Sang Om Sorg Och Gladje
1974 Golliwog/Here For You're Love
1975 Dom Har Glomt/Gulleplutt
1975 SOS/Visa I Attonde Manaden
1979 Nar Du Tar Mig I Din Famn/Jag Var Sa Kar
1982 Never Again (Duet with Tomas Ledin)
1982 Ya Nunca Mas (Duet with Tomas Ledin)
1983 The Heat Is On/Man
1983 The Heat Is On/Man *(Picture disc release)*
1983 Wrap Your Arms Around Me/Take Good Care Of Your Children
1983 Can't Shake Loose/To Love
1983 Can't Shake Loose/To Love *(Picture disc release)*
1983 It's So Nice To Be Rich/P & B
1985 I Won't Let You Go/You're There
1985 One Way Love/Turn The World Around
1986 The Way You Are/Fly Like The Eagle (Duet with Ola Hakansson)
1987 Karusellvisan -Liteen & Trott (with Christian)
1987 Pa Sondag/Mitt Namn Ar Blom (with Christian)
1988 The Last Time/Are You Gonna Throw It All Away
1988 I Wasn't The One Who Said Goodbye/If You Need Somebody Tonight
1988 Let It Shine /Maybe It Was Magic

AGNETHA FALTSKOG ALBUM RELEASES

1968 Agentha Faltskog
1969 Agentha Faltskog Volume 2
1970 Som Jag Ar
1971 Nar En Vacker Blir En Sang
1973 Basta
1974 Agnetha
1975 Elva Kvinnor I Ett Hus
1979 Tio Ar Med Agnetha
1980 Nu Tandas Tusen Juleljus *(Christmas album with Linda)*
1983 Wrap Your Arms Around Me
1985 Eyes Of A Woman
1986 Sjung Denna Sang
1987 Kom Fojl Med I Var Karusell *(Children's album with Christian)*
1988 I Stand Alone

ANNI-FRID LYNGSTAD – SINGLE RELEASES
1967 En Ledig Dag/Peter Kom Tilbaka
1967 Din/Due Ar Sa Underbart Rar
1968 Simsalabim/Vi Mots Ingen
1968 Mycket Kar/nar Du Blir Min
1969 Harlig Ar Var Jord/Rakna De Lychliga Stunderna
1969 Sa Sund Du Masta Ga/Forsok Och Sov Pa Saken
1969 Peter Pan/Du Betonar Karlek Lite Fel
1970 Dar Du Gar Lamnar Karkleken Spar/Du Var Framling Har Igar
1971 En Liten Sang Om Karlek/Tre Kvart Fran Nu
1971 En Kvall En Sommarm/Vi Vet Alt Men Nastan Inget
1971 Min Egen Stad/En Gang Ar Ingen Gang
1972 Kom Och Sjung En Sang/Vi Ar Alla Bara I Borjan
1972 Vad Gor Jag Med Min Karlek/Alting Ska Bli Bra
1972 Man Vill Ju Leva Lite Drssemellan/Ska Man Skratta Eller Grata
1975 Fernando/Ett Live I Solen
1982 I Know There's Something Going On/Threnody
1982 Strip – with Adam Ant
1983 I Turn The Stone/I've Got Something
1983 Here We'll Stay/Strangers
1983 Belle – with Daniel Balavoine
1983 Time – with B. A. Robertson
1984 Shine/That's Tough
1984 Come To Me/Slowly
1987 Sa Langa Vi Har Varamn (with Ratata)
1987 As Long As I Have You (with Ratata)
1992 Anglamark/Saltwater

ANNI-FRID – ALBUM RELEASES
1971 Frida
1972 Min Egen Stad
1976 Ensam
1982 Something's Going On
1984 Shine
1991 Pa Egen Hand

A183A